# Making It

## Manufacturing Techniques for Product Design

Laurence King Publishing

For Jerome, our treasure

LAURENCE KING

This book has been produced by
Central Saint Martins Book Creation,
Southampton Row, London WC1B 4AP, UK

Laurence King Publishing Ltd
361–373 City Road
London EC1V 1LR
United Kingdom
Tel: + 44 20 7841 6900
Fax: + 44 20 7841 6910
e-mail: enquiries@laurenceking.co.uk
www.laurenceking.co.uk

A catalogue record for this book is available
from the British Library

ISBN-13: 978-1-85669-506-0
ISBN-10: 1 85669-506-9

670   LEF

Designed by Roger Fawcett-Tang, Struktur Design
Cover design by Pentagram
Edited by Jessica Spencer
Picture research by Anna Frohm and Ishbel Neat
Printed in China

Frontispiece: plasma-arc cutting; courtesy of TWI

# Contents

# Introduction

Most of us are drawn to the unknown. We like to uncover secrets and that includes looking behind the scenes of modern manufacturing. From early childhood, we have all been intrigued by the TV shows that enable us to peer through the windows of factories to look at lines of chocolate biscuits or milk bottles being made. Tourists increasingly like to support cottage industries in the regions they are visiting, watching live demonstrations of the craftsmen's art. We even find DVD 'bonus features' compelling as they reveal how filmmakers cheat reality with special effects. Designers constantly look beyond the obvious; we like to take technologies, both new and old, and transform them by applying them in innovative ways.

The aim of this book is to explore the hidden 'back story' of manufactured objects from the point of view of industrial product design. *Making It* will enable designers to peer into the world of machines, de-mystifying the manufacturing processes that are used, often in creative – even inspired – ways, to 'morph' liquids, solids, sheets, powders and hunks of metal into three-dimensional products. Other books on this subject tend to present information from a manufacturing or engineering point of view, but technical manuals, trade journals, and websites for associations and federations in the engineering sectors can be unsympathetic to the way designers operate.

This is an age in which old ideas of manufacturing are being re-evaluated by the design industry and new possibilities are surfacing almost daily. These have the potential to dramatically alter the way we make, choose and consume our products. It used to be the case that design was the slave of manufacturing, with creativity restricted for a whole host of reasons (not least moulding constraints and cost). Although, in most instances, this remains the case, manufacturing is increasingly becoming another tool in the designer's toolbox. As well as looking at the long-established manufacturing processes with which designers may already be acquainted, *Making It* reveals how, through experimentation and innovation, the designer's repertoire is being added to continually in terms of the range of materials, production volumes and manufacturing bases available.

*Making It* deals predominantly with mass-production techniques, some of them well established, others very new. For these 'tools' to be used effectively, they need to be understood in all their forms and to be presented in a manner that is relevant to design. They must stimulate ideas and allow for new creative connections to be made, connections that could provoke the appropriating of a technology into a new area or industry.

The wide range of more than 90 processes is broken into chapters based on the way a product designer might approach manufacturing. Consequently, the processes are grouped according to the sorts of shapes they make: so, Chapter 1 describes making things by cutting away at a solid material to form a shape; Chapter 2, the techniques that involve cutting shapes from sheet material, and so on.

Only in Chapter 7 does this categorisation change: it describes advanced processes, including some that abduct a technology from a completely different field and apply it in unexpected ways, and others that use more than one technology.

I do not expect this book to be read from start to finish. Related topics are comprehensively cross-referenced to help readers navigate their way around the material as they dip in and out. The processes range from large-scale industrial mass production, through smaller, almost craft-like production, to the nano-scale production that is carried out in laboratory-like conditions. The product images that illustrate the processes may grab your attention as you flick through, but the exciting thing is that these are only a 'taster' of what is achievable using a particular method.

Familiarity with the contents of this book should lead to confidence and a willingness to push the limits. There is a continued value, nevertheless, in the simple processes, such as jiggering and jollying (see Chapter 1, 'Cut from Solid', on p.23), not least because they serve to debunk the mystery of manufacturing. From there, it is just a small step to understanding advanced processes including rapid prototyping using stereolithography, or contour crafting, which can build a house by spraying concrete in a pattern determined by a CAD file (both Chapter 7, 'Advanced', pp.218 and 216 respectively).

Modern technology is having a profound effect not only on the materials that can be employed, but also on the scale of production and the locations in which 'manufacturing' can now take place. To an extent, this relies on designers being able to control both the design and the means of production. The experimentation of designers such as Tom Dixon (see Chapter 3, 'Continuous', extrusion on p.78) is a case in point – he has borrowed the output of mass-production (extruded plastic) and produced tables that can be described as new 'craft' objects, though they are produced not in a studio or workshop but in a factory.

Tom Dixon's work reveals how new tools available to designers are not necessarily physical tools in the old sense, but factory set-ups in which the machines themselves are used for experimentation. Consider also Malcolm Jordan's Curvy Composites, a degree-show design project that resulted in a completely new way of forming wood (see Chapter 5, 'Into Solid', inflating wood on p.166).

I couldn't resist including some of the more offbeat processes, including inflating metal (see Chapter 2, 'Sheet', p.62) and the interpretation by Tom Vaughan and William Smith of rotational moulding (see Chapter 4, 'Thin and Hollow', p.119), that do not really fit into the category of the mass-produced object, but help point the way to a new direction. Some forms of industrial production can be combined with a craft-like approach, resulting in projects that take small-scale, widely available machines and re-use them for different ends.

Before the Industrial Revolution, output of crafted objects was largely determined by geography. Ceramics were designed and made in areas where there was an abundance of clay – it is no coincidence that Stoke-on-Trent, in the north west of England, was the home of Wedgwood and countless other ceramics factories. Areas with abundant woodland led to the establishment of furniture-making communities. Materials were a local resource and skills evolved gradually and were handed down. The Industrial Revolution helped to bring about a global economy that has, in recent years, broken the link between the source of materials and the local communities, and increasingly manufacturing has tended to take place wherever labour is cheapest.

Now, however, technology is enabling the small-scale craft user to reassert control over certain production methods; it can also place some of them directly in the hands of the consumer.

Reusing existing products or technologies is a vital part of our evolution: experimenting, mixing things up and swapping them around, using this for that, and generally turning existing conventions on their head. From animal husbandry to GM farming and the cloning of animals, we have, it seems, an insatiable appetite for making things race ahead at full speed. But whereas in the past hand tools were used for shaping materials, the new tools of the craftsman are the machines. For a reasonably small sum, you can buy an inkjet printer, take out the guts and start playing with the workings and use CAD-driven data to produce a whole range of new things. Who would have thought that the humble printer could have been used for building human tissue (see Chapter 7, 'Advanced', ink-jet printing on p.214)? When people first started making 'things' they picked up a lump of wood, understood its properties (to a certain degree) and were able to chop it or cut it into a usable product. For some, the lump of wood has become the ink-jet printer, a piece of technology that has been chopped up and generally messed about with, that has the potential to create a multitude of products.

## How to use this book

*Making It* is divided into chapters based on the shapes of components that can be produced using the methods under discussion. It does not set out to answer every question you will ever ask about these methods, but provides a clear and straightforward introduction to each process using a combination of text, diagrams and photographs of the products and some of the manufacturing processes themselves. The visual explanations provided in the diagrams serve to encapsulate the principles of the process and the steps that go into making a final component. They are not meant to be accurate drawings of the machines.

You will notice that there are variations in the headings for some of the processes. These fall into three different categories: those processes that can be identified by another name (hence, AKA, or 'also known as'); those for which the title given is more of an umbrella term – 'machining', for example, includes many techniques (turning, boring, facing, drilling, reaming, milling and turning); the final category is those where two or more processes have been combined, indicated by the word 'with'.

The text for each feature is broken down into three elements: introductory text, an information box, and pros (+) and cons (–). The introductory text gives an overview of the process, its workings and its most notable features and, if appropriate, places it in its context within a particular field of manufacturing. The handy pros (+) and cons (–) feature consists of bullet-pointed notes summarising each production method, and containing many of the key features of the process at a glance. In the yellow information box there is a summary of the particular qualities and characteristics of that process. The information is, for each process, broken down under the following headings:

### Volumes of production

This explains the range of unit volumes that different methods are capable of, from one-off rapid prototyping to hundreds of thousands within a single production run.

### Unit price vs capital investment

One of the main criteria for a designer when it comes to specifying a particular method of production is knowing the initial investment that is required. This can vary enormously, from plastic-forming methods (such as the various forms of injection moulding discussed in Chapter 4, 'Thin and Hollow', see p.111), which can cost tens of thousands of pounds, to CAD-driven methods (featured throughout the book, but especially in Chapter 7, 'Advanced') which require no tooling and very minimal set-up costs.

## Speed

The number of units that can be produced over a period of time is an important factor influencing the designer's choice of process. If, for example, you want to make 10,000 glass bottles, then the automated glass blow moulding process (blow and blow moulding, see Chapter 4, 'Thin and Hollow', p.103), which can produce 15,000 pieces per hour, would not be for you, as the set-up and tooling costs would be prohibitive for such a short amount of time spent on the machines.

## Surface

This briefly describes the type of surface finish you can expect from a particular process.This can, of course, vary enormously but it does give a clue to whether a secondary process will be needed to arrive at a finished part.

## Types/complexity of shape

This particular area offers guidance on any restrictions that will affect the shape of the component and any design details that need to be considered.

## Scale

This gives an indication of the scale of the products that can be produced using the particular process. This section contains some surprising facts, for example, that some metal spinners can spin metal sheets up to 3.5 metres in diameter (see Chapter 2, 'Sheet', metal spinning on p.48).

## Tolerances

The degree of accuracy that a process is capable of achieving is often determined by the material. Machine-cut metals or injection-moulded plastics, for example, are capable of highly controlled tolerances. Certain ceramic processes, on the other hand, are much less able to achieve precise finished dimensions. This section gives examples of this accuracy.

## Relevant Materials

This is simply a short list of the types, or ranges, of materials that can be formed using the featured process.

## Typical applications

A list of products that typically utilise the method of production. The word 'typical' is used advisedly, as the list is not exhaustive but gives sufficient examples to help explain the process.

## Similar methods

This provides clear cross-references to other processes featured in the book, that might be looked at as an alternative form of production to the one featured.

## Further information

This lists web resources to visit for further information. These include contributors to the book. Any relevant associations, where available, are also listed.

As with any specialist field, the world of manufacturing has its own unique vocabulary – this amounts to a huge list of descriptions specific to particular areas of manufacturing. The glossary at the end of the book provides a list of some of these technical terms, with a short definition. Its contents assumes a degree of knowledge of common terms that designers would already know and does not include these.

The book has been carefully cross-referenced throughout to make it easy to find any processes that are being referred to elsewhere. There is, nevertheless, also an index that contains specific materials, companies, designers, and so on.

# 1:
# Cut fro
# Solid

## The use of cutting tools to sculpt materials

This chapter encompasses some of the oldest processes used in the
manufacture of objects, and these processes can be quite simply
categorised by the fact that they use tools that cut away, shape and
remove material. Increasingly, the 'brutal' part of these processes
is being performed by automated CAD-driven machines, which
effortlessly carve through most materials, providing yet another
avenue for the exploitation of rapid prototyping technology and
the replacement of the craftsman who gave life to many products
throughout history.

# Machining

including turning, boring, facing, drilling, reaming, milling and broaching

Machining belongs to a branch of production that falls under the commonly used umbrella term 'chip-forming' (meaning any cutting technique that produces 'chips' of material as a result of the cut). All machining processes have in common the fact that they involve cutting in one form or another. Machining is also used as a post-forming method, as a finishing method and for adding secondary details such as threads.

The term 'machining' itself embraces many different processes. These include several forms of lathe operation for cutting metals, such as turning, boring, facing and threading, all of which involve a cutter being brought to the surface of the rotating material. Turning (see also p.20) generally refers to cutting the outside surface, while boring refers to cutting an internal cavity. Facing uses the cutter to cut into the flat end of the rotating work piece. It is used to clean up the end face, but the same tool can be used to remove excess material. Threading is a process that uses a

| Product | Mini Maglite® torch |
|---|---|
| Designer | Anthony Maglica |
| Materials | aluminium |
| Manufacturer | Maglite Instruments Inc. |
| Country | USA |
| Date | 1979 |

The Maglite® torch, with its highly distinctive engineered aesthetic, has been produced using a number of metal chip-forming techniques, notably turning. The textured pattern for the grip, however, is produced post forming using a process known as knurling.

## Volumes of production

These vary according to type, but computer numerical control (CNC)-automated milling and turning production involves several cutters working on several parts at the same time, which can result in reasonably high volumes of production. This large collection of techniques also includes hand machining of individual components.

## Unit price vs capital investment

In general, there are no tooling costs involved, but the mounting and unmounting of work from the machine reduces production rates. However, the process can still be economical for short runs. CNC-automated milling and turning use CAD files to automate the process and produce complex shapes, which can be batched or mass-produced. Although standard cutters can be used for most jobs, specific cutters may need to be produced, which would drive up overall costs.

## Speed

Varies depending on the specific process.

## Surface

Machining involves polishing, to a degree, and it is possible to achieve excellent results without the need for post forming. Cutters can also produce engineered, ultra-flat surfaces.

## Types/complexity of shape

Work produced on a lathe dictates that parts are axisymmetric, since the work piece is rotated around a fixed centre. Milled parts start life as a block of metal and allow for much more complex components to be formed.

## Scale

Machined components range in size from watch components up to large-scale turbines.

## Tolerances

Machined materials can deliver exceptionally high levels of tolerance: ±0.01 millimetre is normal.

## Relevant materials

Machining is generally applied to metals, but plastics, glass, wood and even ceramics also make use of the machining process. In the case of ceramics, there are certain glass ceramics that are specifically designed to be machined and allow for new forms of processing ceramics. Macor is a particularly well-known brand. Mycalex, a glass-bonded mica by the US-based company Mykroy, is another machinable ceramic that eliminates the need for firing.

## Typical products

Unique parts for industry – pistons, screws, turbines and a mass of other small and large parts for different industries. Alloy car wheels are often put on a lathe to finish the surface.

## Similar methods

The term 'machining' encompasses such a wide set of processes that it is a family of methods in itself, but you could consider dynamic lathing (p.20) as an alternative to conventional lathing.

## Further information

www.pma.org
www.nims-skills.org
www.khake.com/page88.html

sharp, serrated tool to create screw threads in a pre-drilled hole.

Drilling and reaming are generally also lathe operations (though they can be also be done on a milling machine, or by hand), but they require different cutters. As with all lathe operations, the work piece is clamped in the centre of a rotating chuck. Whereas drilling is a straightforward operation to create a hole, reaming involves enlarging an existing hole to a smooth finish, which is done with a special reaming tool that has several cutting edges.

Other machining processes include milling and broaching. Milling involves a rotating cutter, similar to a drill, which is often used to cut into a metal surface (though it can be applied to just about any other solid material). Broaching is a process used to create holes, slots and other complex internal features (such as the internal shape of a spanner head, after it has been forged, see p.169).

1  A very simple set-up for milling a chunk of metal. The cutting tool, which resembles a flat drill bit, can be seen fitted above the clamped work piece.

2  A straightforward set-up for a lathe operation in which the tube of metal to be cut is clamped into a chuck. The cutter is poised ready to make a cut.

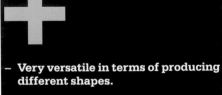

**+**

- Very versatile in terms of producing different shapes.
- Can be applied to virtually any solid material.
- High degree of accuracy.

**−**

- Can be slow.
- Parts can be restricted to the stock sizes of material used.
- Low material utilisation due to wastage when cutting.

# Computer Numerical Controlled (CNC) Cutting

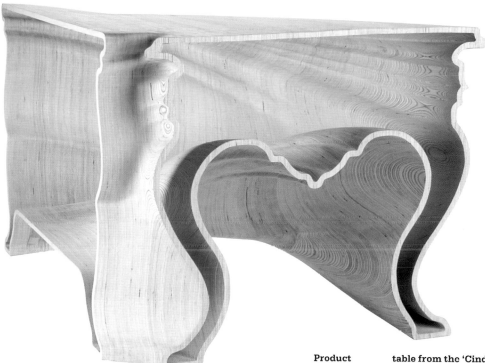

| Product | table from the 'Cinderella' range |
|---|---|
| Designer | Jeroen Verhoeven |
| Materials | Finnish birch plywood |
| Manufacturer | Demakersvan |
| Country | Holland |
| Date | 2004 |

The way computer numerical controlled (CNC) machines effortlessly cut through solid materials as if they were butter is almost sublime. The cutting heads are mounted onto a head that rotates in up to six axes, to chisel different forms as if they were automated robotic sculptors.

    Designed by Jeroen Verhoeven, a member of the Dutch design group Demakersvan, the piece of furniture featured here is as multi-layered in meaning as it is in its construction.

The surreal construction and shape of this table from the 'Cinderella' range fits perfectly with the manufacturer's belief that high-tech machines are our hidden Cinderellas. The table is a witty play on traditional, romantic furniture made using a thoroughly modern manufacturing process.

As Demakersvan puts it, 'The big miracle of how industrial products come about is a wonderful phenomenon if you look at it closely. The high-tech machines are our hidden Cinderellas. We make them work in robot lines, while they can be so much more.'

This thought is put into practice in the production of its Cinderella table (pictured). The table is made up of 57 layers of birch multiplex, which are individually cut, glued and then cut again with a CNC machine. The table exemplifies perfectly the ability of multi-axis CNC machines to carve away at three-dimensional forms in a highly intricate manner, using information from a CAD file. It is also a unique example of a totally new form: created from an ancient material in a process that can cut virtually any shape from a piece of material, this table goes some way to reveal what Demakersvan describes as the 'secrets hidden in high-tech production techniques'.

## Volumes of production

CNC cutting is best suited to one-off or batch production because of the slow progress rate.

## Unit price vs capital investment

No tooling, just the expensive time for cutting and the creation, using CAD, of the three-dimensional data.

## Speed

The speed is determined by several factors, including the material, the complexity of the form and the surface finish that is required.

## Surface

Good, but may require some post finishing, depending on the material.

## Types/complexity of shape

Virtually any shape that can be conceived on a computer screen.

## Scale

From small components to huge objects. CNC Auto Motion in the US, for example, is one of several companies manufacturing monster-sized machines having over 15 metres of travel, with 3 metres of vertical-axis travel and a gantry measuring 6 metres across.

## Tolerances

High.

## Relevant materials

CNC technology can be used for cutting a wide range of materials, including wood, metal, plastic, granite and marble. It can also be used for cutting foam and modelling clay (see below).

## Typical products

Ideally suited for making complex bespoke designs such as injection-moulding tools, die cutters, furniture components and the highly crafted, complex forms of handrails. It can also be used, in automotive design studios, for rapid prototyping of full-size cars in foam or modelling clay.

## Similar methods

Laser cutting (p.40) when the laser is mounted on a multi-axis head is possibly the closest method.

## Further information

www.demakersvan.com
www.haldeneuk.com
www.cncmotion.com
www.tarus.com

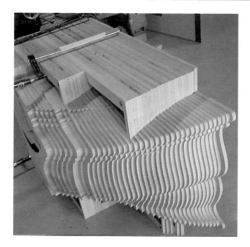

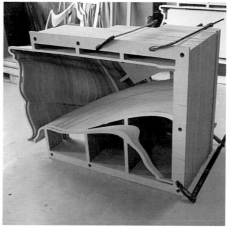

1  The individual sheets of cut plywood are clamped together before being machined.

2  View showing the machined internal structure before the external surface is cut.

**+**

- Can be used on virtually any material.

- Designs can be cut straight from CAD files.

- Highly adaptable for cutting intricate and complex shapes.

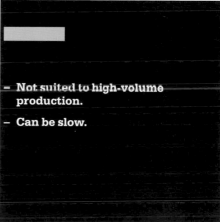

**–**

- Not suited to high-volume production.

- Can be slow.

# Electron-Beam Machining (EBM)

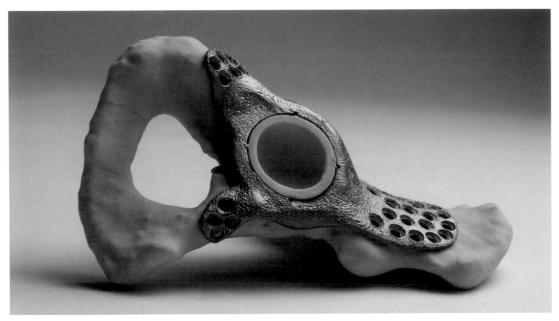

Electron-Beam Machining (EBM) is a versatile process that is used to cut, weld, drill or anneal components. As a machining process, one of its many advantages is that ultra-fine cuts can be made with such high precision that they can be measured in microns. EBM involves a high-energy beam of electrons being focused by a lens and fired at extremely high speeds (between 50 and 80 per cent of the speed of light) onto a specific area of the component, causing the material to heat up, melt and vaporise. The process needs to occur in a vacuum chamber to ensure that the electrons are not disrupted and thrown off course by air molecules.

| Product | customised tri-flange implants |
|---|---|
| Materials | titanium |
| Country | Sweden |
| Date | 2005 |

This titanium hip-bone plate illustrates the spattered surface that is a common result of this process.

## Volumes of production

Suited to one-off or batch production.

## Unit price vs capital investment

Low capital investment as there are no tooling costs because the pattern is driven by a CAD file. However, the electron-beam equipment itself is very expensive.

## Speed

The beam of electrons moves at a very high velocity, so cutting speeds are fast. For example, a hole of up to 125 microns in diameter can be cut almost instantly in a sheet 1.25 millimetres thick. Naturally, the type of material and its thickness affects the cycle time. In order to make a 100 millimetre-wide slot in a piece of stainless steel 0.175 millimetres thick, cutting will occur at a rate of 50 millimetres per minute. The implant (shown here) took four hours to produce.

## Surface

The process can cause various surface markings that, depending on the application, might not be desirable, such as spattering close to the cut.

## Types/complexity of shape

The process is ideally suited to cutting fine lines of holes in thin materials. The beam can be focused to 10 to 200 microns, which means that costs are justified by an extremely high degree of accuracy.

## Scale

The disadvantage of using a vacuum chamber is that part sizes are limited.

## Tolerances

Extremely high, with cuts as fine as 10 microns possible. With materials over 0.13 millimetres thick, the cut will have a fine, two-degree taper.

## Relevant materials

Virtually any material, although materials that have high melting temperatures slow down the process.

## Typical products

Apart from engineering applications and the medical implant shown here, one of the more interesting uses for EBM is for joining carbon nanotubes. Joining anything on the nano-scale is difficult, but because there is no contact with the material, EBM provides a method of joining the tubes together in a way that does not crush them.

## Similar methods

Laser cutting (p.40) and plasma-arc cutting (p.27).

## Further information

www.arcam.com
www.sodick.de

**+**

- Highly accurate.

- There is no contact with the material being cut, so it therefore requires minimal clamping.

- Can be used for small batches.

- Versatile: a single tool can cut, weld and/or anneal at the same time.

**–**

- A disadvantage compared with laser cutting (see p.40) is that it requires a vacuum chamber.

- Laser cutting can be just as effective for less accurate machining.

- High energy consumption.

# Turning
## with dynamic lathing

The process of mounting a material on a spinning wheel and skimming off thin slices is thousands of years old. The commonly used material for turning is wood, but 'green' ceramic is also highly popular for industrially producing the same types of round, symmetrical shape.

In ceramic turning, a clay is blended into a ceramic body and extruded into something called a 'pug'. This leather-hard, clay lump is mounted onto a lathe and turned, either by hand or with an automated cutter.

At the other end of the industrial production scale, engineers at Germany's Fraunhofer Institute have developed a process called dynamic lathe for producing non-axisymmetric metal parts for engineering applications, without the need to remove and replace the component manually. Shapes are defined by a CAD program and fed directly to a lathe that allows the cutter to move up and down in the lateral axis.

| Product | pestle |
|---|---|
| Materials | ceramic stoneware, with wooden handle |
| Manufacturer | Wade Ceramics |
| Country | UK |

The turning process has been used for both parts of this pestle, the wooden handle and the ceramic grinder head.

### Volumes of production

From single pieces upwards. The costs of tooling and set-up for a single piece can be prohibitive, but this depends on specific requirements. For large quantities, an automated process may be required. The dynamic lathe is currently still in its infancy and is best suited to small production runs or one-offs.

### Unit price vs capital investment

Depends on volume, but low in comparison to other ceramic production methods, such as hot or cold isostatic pressing (see pp.152 and 154) and slip casting (see p.122). In the dynamic lathe method there is no tooling, which obviously keeps costs down.

### Speed

Depends on the product. As an example, a simple candlestick will take 45 seconds, a mortar 1 minute and a pestle 50 seconds. The relationship between the length and depth of the cut in the dynamic-lathe technique determines the speed at which parts can be made. The more peaks with larger depths there are, the slower the process is.

### Surface

Fine surface, but dependent on the material (for example, the wooden handle is less fine than the ceramic head of the pestle shown here).

### Types/complexity of shape

Restricted to symmetrical shapes. Dynamic lathes are a marked improvement on conventional turning on a metalwork lathe, and can produce far more complex parts than might traditionally have been made by casting.

### Scale

A standard maximum size, as produced by Wade Ceramics in the UK, for example, is 350 millimetres in diameter by 600 millimetres in length. A maximum length of 300 millimetres with a maximum working diameter of 350 millimetres is possible with the dynamic-lathe method.

### Tolerances

Tolerance ±2 per cent or 0.2 millimetres, whichever is the greater. However, this is higher when cutting metal on a lathe, especially if using CNC (computer numerical control). For dynamic lathe the tolerance is ±1 millimetre.

### Relevant materials

Ceramics and wood are common materials for turning, however just about any solid material can be cut in this way. Most metals and plastics can be used for the dynamic-lathe process, although hard carbon steels can be problematic.

### Typical products

Bowls, plates, door handles, pestles, ceramic electrical insulators and furniture.

### Similar methods

For ceramics, a similar type of rotating set-up is used in both jiggering and jollying (p.23).

### Further information

www.wade.co.uk

www.fraunhofer.de/fhg/EN/press/pi/
  2005/09/Mediendienst92005
  Thema3.jsp?print=true

1  The mortar bowl is being turned by hand, using a profiled metal tool to achieve a precise profile.

2  A ceramic pestle being finished using a flat smoothing tool.

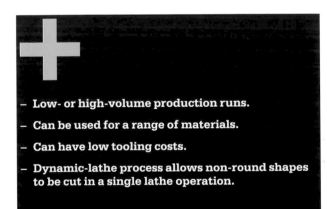

- Low- or high-volume production runs.
- Can be used for a range of materials.
- Can have low tooling costs.
- Dynamic-lathe process allows non-round shapes to be cut in a single lathe operation.

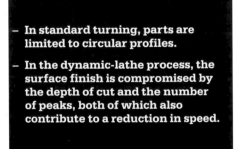

- In standard turning, parts are limited to circular profiles.
- In the dynamic-lathe process, the surface finish is compromised by the depth of cut and the number of peaks, both of which also contribute to a reduction in speed.

# Jiggering and Jollying

Jiggering and jollying are two profoundly silly words that describe similar methods for the mass-production of ceramic hollow shapes, such as bowls, or flatter shapes, such as plates. The easiest way to get a sense of these methods is to think of hand throwing on a potter's wheel, but turned into an industrial process where the craftsman's hands are replaced by a profiled cutter, which scrapes the clay as it rotates on the wheel. In jiggering, the mould determines the internal form of the shape while the cutter forms the outer shape, while in jollying the cutter forms the inner shape.

Jollying is employed to make deep shapes, the first stage of which involves extruding a clay slug that is cut into discs and used to form liners. These are like clay cups that are formed to be of similar proportions to the final piece. The liners are placed inside the cup moulds, which are fitted to a rotating spindle on the jollying wheel. This is where the similarity to hand throwing comes in. On the rotating spindle, the clay is drawn up the inside of the mould, forming the wall. A profiled head is then brought down

| Product | Wedgwood plate |
|---|---|
| Materials | bone china |
| Manufacturer | Wedgwood |
| Country | UK |
| Date | 1920 |

This classic design from the Wedgwood stable is produced using jiggering, a process that has altered little since the foundation of Josiah Wedgwood's pottery in 1759, except for the introduction of electricity to power the wheel. Turn any such plate upside down and you see the shape of the cutting profile used to scrape away the clay.

into the cup to scrape away the clay and form the finished and precise inside profile.

Jiggering is a very similar process to jollying but is used to form shallow rather than deep shapes. It works in an inside-out way to jollying, because the shaped profile cuts the outside surface rather than the inside. Again, a slug of clay is formed and placed over a rotating mould, known as a 'spreader'. Here, it is formed into an even thickness by a flat profile. This thick pancake, which is known as a 'bat', is removed and placed onto the plate mould. The mould forms the inside shape of the plate. The whole thing rotates and a profile is brought down to scrape away the external side of the clay and form a precise, uniform outside shape.

### Volumes of production
Can be used for both batch and mass-production. Many of the big potteries use these methods as a standard way of producing bowls and plates.

### Unit price vs capital investment
Affordable tooling for batch production. The process can also be used for small runs of handmade production.

### Speed
Jollying produces an average of eight pieces per minute, jiggering an average of four units per minute.

### Surface
The surface finish is such that the products can be glazed and fired without any intermediate finishing.

### Types/complexity of shape
Compared with slip casting (see p.122), where the detail on the inside wall of a piece is totally dependent on the outside form, these two processes allow total control over both the inside and outside profiles individually.

### Scale
The standard size for machine-made dinner plates is up to a fired diameter of approximately 30 centimetres.

### Tolerances
± 2 millimetres.

### Relevant materials
All types of ceramic.

### Typical products
Both methods are principally used for producing tableware and are distinguished by the depth of the shapes they produce. Jollying is used to make products such as pots, cups and bowls, which are generally deep containers, while jiggering is used to make shallow items such as plates, saucers and shallow bowls.

### Similar methods
Apart from using a potter's wheel, the closest ceramic alternative to jiggering and jollying is turning (p.20), which can be used to make symmetrical shapes and different profiles without a large investment in tooling (although it requires a more complex set-up). Alternative methods also include cold and hot isostatic pressing (pp.152 and 154) and pressure-assisted slip casting (p.122).

### Further information
www.wades.co.uk
www.royaldoulton.com

## Jiggering

bat

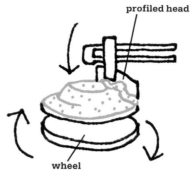

profiled head

mould

wheel

1  In jiggering, a thick, even pancake of clay (known as a 'bat') is placed over a mould, which forms the inside shape of the plate.

2  A profiled head is brought down onto the rotating bat to scrape away the clay, to make a precise, external profile.

3  The finished soup bowl, ready for firing.

1  A slug of clay is placed on a spreader.

2  A flat profile forms it into an even 'bat'.

3  The bat is transferred by hand from the spreader.

4  Manual placement of the bat onto the mould.

5  The profiled head, closely supervised, acts against the rotating bat to scrape away the clay.

6  Typical of the sort of flat shape produced by jiggering, these soup bowls are now ready for firing.

## Jollying

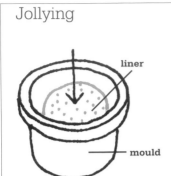
liner

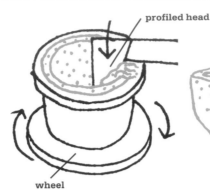
profiled head

mould

wheel

**1** In jollying, a clay slug is extruded and cut into discs to form liners. Each liner is placed inside a cupped mould, fitted to a rotating spindle on a wheel.

**2** Clay is drawn up the inside of the mould, forming the wall. A profiled head scrapes away the clay to make the precise inside profile.

**3** The finished bowl, ready for firing.

**1** A rough disc (liner) is pressed into a deep mould.

**2** A profiled head spreads the liner evenly around the inside of the rotating mould.

**3** Hand finishing of the outer surface, the side that was in contact with the mould.

**+**

– Allows complete control of the thicknesses and shapes of sections.

– Can be more cost-effective than slip casting (see p.122).

– Less prone to distortion than cast pots.

**–**

– Can be inaccurate due to shrinkage during firing.

– Because these processes both work on the potter's-wheel principle, they are only able to produce symmetrical parts.

# Plasma-Arc Cutting

'Men in overalls wearing dark view-control helmets' is perhaps all I need to say to sum up this process. Along with oxyacetylene cutting (see p.42), plasma-arc cutting lives in the land of heavy industry, and it is part of the non-chip-forming branch of production known as thermal cutting. It works by means of a stream of ionised gas, which becomes so hot that it will literally vaporise the metal that is being cut.

The process takes its name from the term 'plasma', which is what a gas turns into when it is heated to a very high level. It involves a stream of gas – usually nitrogen, argon, or oxygen – being sent through a small channel at the centre of a nozzle, which at its heart contains a negatively charged electrode. The combination of power supplied to this electrode, and contact between the tip of the nozzle and the metal being cut, results in a circuit being created. This produces a powerful spark, the arc, between the electrode and the metal work piece,

This shows the heavy, industrial nature of this particular cutting method. The tube is rotated around the central axis to allow for a short length to be removed.

which heats the gas to its plasma state. The arc can reach temperatures as high as 27,800°C and it therefore melts the metal as the nozzle passes over it.

The cutting line width, known as the 'kerf', needs to be considered when designing certain shapes because its thickness can range from 1 to 4 millimetres, depending on the thickness of the metal plate, and can affect the dimensions of the component.

### Volumes of production

Plasma-arc cutting is an economical process for small-batch quantities because it can be performed without tooling.

### Unit price vs capital investment

Unless a cutting template is introduced, the process does not require tooling. In the automated process, the information for the shape is provided by CAD files.

### Speed

There is generally very little set-up time involved, but the speed is greatly affected by the type of material and its thickness. For example, to cut a 25 millimetre chunk of steel, 300 millimetres long, will take about one minute, whereas a 2 millimetre piece can be cut at a rate of 2,400 millimetres per minute.

### Surface

Even when hard stainless steel is used, the process provides smooth, clean edges with better results than those produced by oxyacetylene cutting (see p.42). The cutting can also be controlled to produce different grades of surface, depending on the cost versus the edge quality – that is, longer cutting times equal better edge finish.

### Types/complexity of shape

The process is best suited to heavy-gauge materials. Thin-gauge metals of below 8 millimetres may distort as a result of the process, as may thin and narrow sections. As in all sheet-cutting operations, nesting one shape within another (as when you make biscuits and cut them as close as possible to make the most of the rolled dough) results in an economical use of the material.

### Scale

Handheld cutting means there is no maximum size. Sheets thinner than about 8 millimetres may distort.

### Tolerances

Depend on the thickness of the material, but, to give a basic idea, it is possible to keep tolerance to ±1.5 millimetres for sheet materials 6–35 millimetres thick.

### Relevant materials

Any electrically conductive metallic material, but most commonly stainless steel and aluminium. The process becomes more difficult the higher the carbon content of the steel.

### Typical products

Heavy construction, including shipbuilding and machine components.

### Similar methods

Electron-beam machining (EBM) (p.18), oxyacetylene cutting (p.42), laser (p.40) and water-jet cutting (p.36).

### Further information

www.aws.org
www.twi.org.uk/j32k/index.xtp
www.iiw-iis.org
www.hypertherm.com
www.centricut.com

# Plasma-arc Cutting

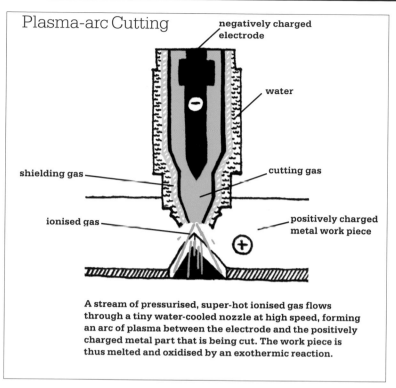

negatively charged electrode

water

shielding gas

cutting gas

ionised gas

positively charged metal work piece

A stream of pressurised, super-hot ionised gas flows through a tiny water-cooled nozzle at high speed, forming an arc of plasma between the electrode and the positively charged metal part that is being cut. The work piece is thus melted and oxidised by an exothermic reaction.

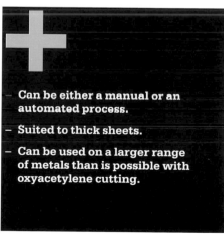

- Can be either a manual or an automated process.
- Suited to thick sheets.
- Can be used on a larger range of metals than is possible with oxyacetylene cutting.

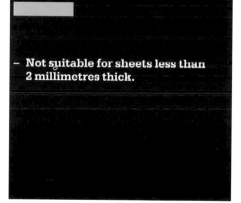

- Not suitable for sheets less than 2 millimetres thick.

# 2:
# Sheet

## Components that start life as a sheet of material

Within the last fifteen years or so, there has been a surge in the
number of products made from sheet material. Maybe this is
because the starting point is a pre-prepared material, which goes
some way in reducing the production costs. Maybe it is also the
cost-effectiveness of die-cutting tools, or even the absence of any
tooling costs for processes such as chemical milling. But, on a
mass-market level, the die cutting of a plastic such as polypropylene
has led to a wealth of new packaging, lighting and even larger-scale
furniture. Perhaps it is also the ability of these materials to be cut
by a manufacturer and handfolded and assembled by the consumer
that has created an appeal.

# Chemical Milling
## AKA Photo-Etching

Chemical milling, also known as photo-etching, is a great method for producing intricate patterns on thin, flat metal sheets by using corrosive acids in a process similar to that used for developing photographs.

Chemical milling involves a resist being printed onto the surface of the material to be treated. This resist works by providing a protective layer against the corrosive action of the acid, and it can be applied in the form of a linear pattern or a photographic image. When the part is sprayed with an acid on both sides, the exposed metal (without the resist) is eaten away by the chemical. As in the die-cutting process (see p.34) used for plastics, crease lines can be 'half-etched' into the pattern which allow the sheet to have foldable crease lines for the creation of three-dimensional structures.

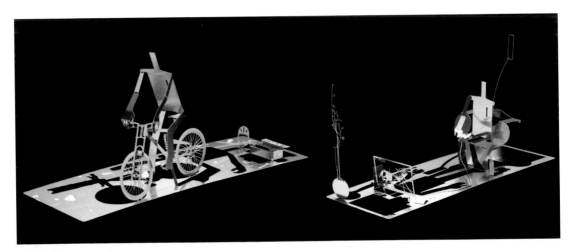

| Product | Mikroman business card |
|---|---|
| Designer | Sam Buxton |
| Materials | stainless steel |
| Date | 2003 |

The fine, intricate details of these cleverly designed business cards, which unfold to show a man on a bicycle and one in an office environment, are an excellent example of the ability of chemical milling to offer a highly decorative and ultra-fine method of cutting metals.

### Volumes of production

Individual pieces can be made, but the process is more suited to batch or mass-production volumes.

### Unit price vs capital investment

The set-up costs involved are low, because the printed resist means there is no need of any hard tooling. However, the unit costs are not likely to be drastically lower for batch items than for mass-produced items.

### Speed

Depends on the complexity of the artwork.

### Surface

Due to the corrosion of the metal, any half-etched surface has a rough and matt texture. However, this texture often becomes a decorative feature. Cut edges are free of burring.

### Types/complexity of shape

The process is ideal for cutting thin sheets and foils. It also allows for highly intricate shapes and details to be cut without any blemishes such as the burn marks that are sometimes caused by laser cutting (see p.40).

### Scale

Generally limited to standard sheet sizes.

### Tolerances

Tolerance levels are determined by the thickness of the material. The holes must be larger (typically 1 to 2 times) than the thickness of the metal, which gives a material with a thickness of between 0.025 and 0.050 millimetres a tolerance of ±0.025 millimetres.

### Relevant materials

A range of metals can be used in the process, including titanium, tungsten and steels.

### Typical products

Electronic components such as switch contacts, actuators, micro screens and graphics for industrial labelling and signs. The process is also used for industrial components, and the military use it to make a flexible trigger device for missiles. The trigger is so fine that it changes according to air pressure the closer it gets to its target.

### Similar methods

Blanking (see metal cutting, p.51), laser cutting (p.40), electron-beam machining (p.18) and electroforming for micro-moulds (p.222).

### Further information

www.rimexmetals.com
www.tech-etch.com
www.precisionmicro.com
www.photofab.co.uk

- No tooling.
- Highly flexible process for creating surface detail.
- The image is laser-plotted onto film from a CAD file, so designs can easily be modified.
- Fine tolerances.
- Suitable for thin sheets.

- Can only be used for metals.

# Die Cutting

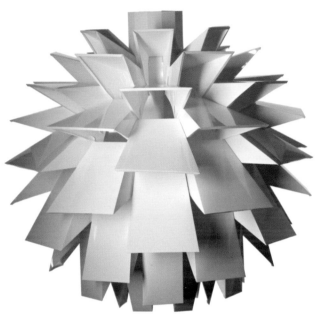

The simplest analogy for this process is to think of a biscuit-cutter for making shapes from dough in the kitchen. Just as easily applied to paper or plastic, die cutting is a simple process that involves a sharp edge being brought down onto a thin material to cut a shape in a single step. A die-cutting tool has two functions: the main function is to cut a shape from the sheet; the second is to apply creases to the material to allow it to form an accurate bend. The creases are necessary when constructing three-dimensional shapes and integrated hinges from a sheet.

| Product | Norm 69 lampshade |
|---|---|
| Designer | Simon Karkov |
| Materials | polypropylene |
| Manufacturer | Normann Copenhagen |
| Country | Denmark |
| Date | 2002 |

The 69 lampshade (above) is sold, flat, in boxes of pizza-size proportions. The flat pieces of die-cut plastic (right) that are contained in the box take the customer about 40 minutes to fold and assemble into this complex structure.

**Volumes of production**

From small batches of around a hundred units, to thousands.

**Unit price vs capital investment**

The low cost of the cutters makes this a highly economical process even for small runs. Sheets of material may be fed individually but if the material comes on a roll there will be a massive reduction in the cost of the final products.

**Speed**

Die cutting is one of the predominant manufacturing processes for packaging, with production cycle times of up to thousands of products per hour. Unlike in moulded products, the cutting speed is not affected by the complexity of the shape. Assembly, however, is more labour-intensive.

**Surface**

The surface is dependent on the material. The cut edge, however, is clean, precise and with a very, very fine radius where the cutter has cut through the material. As you might expect, the sheets can be finished with various forms of printing or embossing, or a combination of the two.

**Types/complexity of shape**

The complexity of the shape is really dependent on the size of the cuts. Very fine slots of less than about 5 millimetres can be difficult to cut. One of the design issues to bear in mind is that the excess plastic around the part needs to be removed and cleaning plastic from fine holes can be difficult.

**Scale**

Most manufacturers should have no problems at all in cutting sheets of up to 1,000 by 700 millimetres, and some are able to go slightly larger and cut straight from a roll. However, material choice is more limited if it comes on a roll. Printing on large sheets, above 1,000 by 700 millimetres, may be difficult due to the limited availability of large-scale printing machines.

**Tolerances**

Very high tolerances.

**Relevant materials**

A large proportion of the material used is polypropylene due to its ability to form a strong integral hinge. Other standard materials include PVC, polyethylene terephthalate (PET), paper and all sorts of card.

**Typical products**

Die cutting is extensively used for packaging, especially boxes and cartons. For this type of product, assembly is required to construct the three-dimensional structures. Other, more product-focused, applications include lampshades that require complex assembly (pictured), toys and even furniture.

**Similar methods**

For cutting flat sheets, try laser (p.40) or water-jet cutting (p.36).

**Further information**

www.burallplastec.com
www.ambroplastics.com
www.bpf.co.uk

- Low set-up costs and cost-effective for batches.
- Can easily be combined with printing.
- Many shapes can be cut in a single cutting action.

- Three-dimensional products need hand assembly and are limited to a set of standard constructions.

# Water-Jet Cutting
## AKA Hydrodynamic Machining

From as early as the mid-nineteenth century, water jets have been used as a method of removing materials during mining. The modern-day process (also known as hydrodynamic machining) has been cranked up to produce an incredibly fine jet of water, typically 0.5 millimetres, which is forced out of a nozzle at a pressure of 20,000–55,000 psi (pounds per square inch) at velocities of up to twice the speed of sound. Water-jet cutting produces a fine cut using water alone, but with an additional abrasive, such as garnet, it can be used to cut through harder materials.

| Product | Prince chair |
|---|---|
| Designer | Louise Campbell |
| Materials | water-cut EPDM (ethylene propylene diene monomer) on laser-cut metal, and felt |
| Manufacturer | Hay |
| Country | Denmark |
| Date | 2005 |

The decorative pattern on this chair illustrates the potential of water-jet cutting to cut intricate patterns into a three-dimensional material.

## Volumes of production

The process involves no tooling and is therefore equally suitable for one-off jobs and large production runs.

## Unit price vs capital investment

Because there is no tooling, and designs are taken from CAD files, set-up costs are low, and there is no consequent hike in unit price. Shapes can also be 'nested' – laid out in a clever way that maximises the surface area of the sheet (as you would when cutting out biscuits from rolled dough).

## Speed

An abrasive jet can cut a 13 millimetre-thick titanium sheet at the rate of 160 millimetres per minute.

## Surface

The cut edge has the same sort of edge as if it had been sand-blasted, but without any of the burring that you may get with laser cutting (see p.40).

## Types/complexity of shape

Because the cutter works like a plotting machine or a CNC router, it is possible to cut fine and intricate shapes. However, due to the high pressure of the water, thin sheet material may distort or bend. Processes such as laser cutting avoid this problem due to the lack of such pressure.

## Scale

Most industrial cutting takes place on a cutting bed, which restricts the size of the material that can be used. Standard sizes extend up to a maximum of 3 by 3 metres. The upper limit for thickness varies with the material.

## Tolerances

The jet can be accurate to 0.1 millimetre. Particularly thick materials may result in the jet 'wandering' slightly from its point of entry.

## Relevant materials

Water-jet cutting offers a huge range of possibilities in terms of materials – you can choose from glass, steel, wood, plastic, ceramics, stone, marble and even paper. It is also used for cutting sandwiches and other food. Having said that, it is worth bearing in mind that materials that are particularly prone to absorbing water are not suited to this process.

## Typical products

Decorative architectural panels and stones. The process works very well under water, and it was used in the rescue operation of the Russian Kursk submarine in 2000.

## Similar methods

The process can be used as an alternative to die cutting (p.34), and as a cold alternative to laser cutting (p.40).

## Further information

www.wjta.org
www.tmcwaterjet.co.uk
www.waterjets.org
www.hay.dk

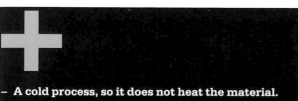

- A cold process, so it does not heat the material.
- No tool contact, therefore no edge deformation.
- Can be used to cut very fine details in a variety of materials of different thicknesses.

- In particularly thick cuts, the jet can move from its original course as it eats into the depth of the material.

# Wire EDM (Electrical Discharge Machining) and Cutting with Ram EDM

In the middle of the first decade of the twenty-first century, designers are rediscovering the use of surface decoration as a valid form of design expression. Industrial techniques have been borrowed from engineering applications and are used to create highly intricate patterns, as decorative as if they have been abstracted from nature or fairy-tale narratives.

Many unusual methods have been invented for cutting complex patterns into difficult materials. Dating back to when the phenomenon was first observed in the 1770s, electricity has been harnessed by scientists for use in cutting and machining materials. Wire EDM (electrical discharge machining) is one of the latest processes to exploit electricity for cutting intricate patterns.

Since its commercial development in the 1970s, wire EDM has become an increasingly popular method of machining metals. Together with processes such as water-jet cutting (see p.36) and laser cutting (see p.40), Wire EDM is a non-contact method of cutting materials. Less commonly used than the other two and more suited to extremely hard steels and other hard-to-cut metals such as high-performance alloys, carbides and titanium, it is, nevertheless, able to achieve the same level of intricacy.

Based on a type of spark-erosion (it is sometimes also referred to as spark machining or spark eroding), wire EDM is used to cut very hard, conductive metals by using sparks to melt away the material. The spark is generated by a thin wire – the electrode – which follows a programmed cutting path (determined by a CAD file). There is no contact between the electrode and the material, so the spark jumps across the gap and melts the material. De-ionised water is simultaneously jetted towards the melting point, cooling the material and washing the waste away.

There is another sort of EDM machine, the 'ram'. As the name suggests, the ram method involves a machined graphite electrode mounted on the end of an arm (the ram) being pushed onto the surface of the material to be cut.

### Volumes of production

The process and shape can be controlled manually by an operator or from a CAD file, so it is equally suited to one-off pieces and automated mass-production.

### Unit price vs capital investment

Requires no tooling.

### Speed

The latest generation of EDM machines can cut up to 400 square millimetres per minute, depending on the electrical resistance of the material and, of course, its thickness. A 50-millimetre piece of steel can be cut at a rate of approximately 4 millimetres per minute.

### Surface

Wire EDM is well known for its ability to achieve an excellent finish.

### Types/complexity of shape

The delicate wire can cut very intricate shapes from the toughest materials.

### Scale

Depending on the material, the generator size and the power, the process can cut through massive hunks of metal up to an astonishing 500 millimetres thick, although this will be very time-consuming, with cutting occurring at a rate of less than 1 millimetre per minute.

### Tolerances

Wire EDM is extremely accurate and can achieve sub-micron tolerances.

### Relevant materials

Restricted to conductive metals. The process is ideally suited to hard metals, the hardness of which does not affect the cutting speed.

### Typical products

One of the big markets for this process is for the super-hardened dies and cutters that are used in industrial production. Other applications include super-tough components for the aerospace industry.

### Similar methods

Laser cutting (p.40) and electron-beam machining (EBM) (p.18).

### Further information

www.precision2000.co.uk
www.sodick.com
www.edmmachining.com

- **Ideal for cutting intricate shapes from metals that would be difficult to machine.**

- **The process cuts without force.**

- **No flushing.**

- **Time-consuming.**

- **Limited to electrically conductive materials.**

# Laser Cutting
## with laser-beam machining

Similar to water-jet cutting (see p.36) and electron-beam machining (see p.18), laser cutting is a non-chip-forming method of cutting and decorating materials. It is a highly accurate process based on input from a CAD file. In a nutshell, it works through a highly focused beam of light generating millions of watts of energy per square centimetre, which melts the material that is in its path.

Laser-beam machining is a form of laser cutting that uses a multi-axis head to cut three-dimensional objects. A CAD file maps complex paths for the powerful beam of light, resulting in fine, accurate designs.

Both of these processes are capable of cutting components that could not be cut precisely with conventional machine tools. As neither method involves contact with the material being cut, minimal clamping is required.

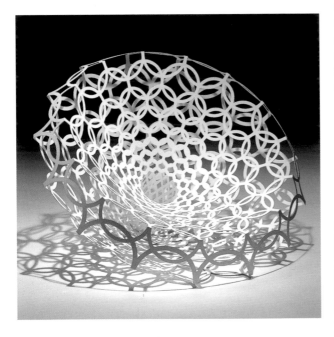

| Product | Very Round Seat |
| --- | --- |
| Designer | Louise Campbell |
| Materials | steel |
| Manufacturer | Zanotta |
| Country | Italy |
| Date | 2006 |

The highly decorative nature of this seat shows a wonderful sensitivity to the possibilities of cutting intricate patterns in hard materials. Its use within the context of furniture design provides a new application area for the process.

1   A typical laser cutting head following a path that is driven by a CAD file.

## Volumes of production

Suited to batch production.

## Unit price vs capital investment

Low capital investment as there is no tooling because the cuts are determined by a CAD file.

## Speed

As with all methods of cutting, the speed of this process is dependent on the type of material used and its thickness. As a rough estimate, titanium alloys between 0.5 and 10 millimetres thick can be cut at a rate of 2.5 to 12 metres per minute.

## Surface

The process will leave burn marks on wood, but on metal can give a clean edge with no need for post finishing. However, metal surfaces should be left unpolished before cutting, as highly polished surfaces act as reflectors and decrease the effectiveness of the process.

## Types/complexity of shape

Depending on the machinery, the laser can be mounted horizontally or on a multi-axis head, allowing for highly complex shapes to be cut in three dimensions, a method that is sometimes called laser-beam machining.

## Scale

Limited to standard sheet sizes.

## Tolerances

Tolerances are extremely high, with holes of as little as 0.025 millimetre in diameter being possible.

## Relevant materials

Often used on hard steels such as stainless and carbon steel. Copper, aluminium, gold and silver are more difficult due to their ability to conduct the heat. Non-metallics can also be laser cut, including woods, paper, plastics and ceramics. Materials such as glass and ceramics are especially suited to laser cutting, since it would be difficult to cut the materials in intricate patterns using any other techniques.

## Typical products

Model components, surgical instruments, wooden toys, metal meshes and filters. Laser-cut ceramics can be used as industrial insulators and furniture can be produced using laser-cut glass or metal.

## Similar methods

Water-jet cutting (p.30), die cutting (p.34), electron-beam machining (EBM) (p.18) and plasma-arc cutting (p.27).

## Further information

www.miwl.org.uk
www.ailu.org.uk
www.precisionmicro.com

---

- No tool wear, minimal clamping and it offers a consistent, highly accurate cut.
- Suited to a range of materials.
- No post treatment of edges.

---

- Has an optimum thickness from which materials can be cut, beyond which you might run into problems.
- Can be time-consuming on large production runs, so it is best suited to one-off or batch production.

# Oxyacetylene Cutting
## AKA Oxygen Cutting, Gas Welding or Gas Cutting

This is a process for cutting metal plate in which oxygen and acetylene are combined at the end of a nozzle and ignited, producing a high-temperature flame. The metal is preheated with this mixture of gases, and then a stream of high-purity oxygen is injected into the centre of the flame, which rapidly oxidises the work piece. Because thermal cutting methods are based on a chemical reaction between the oxygen and iron (or titanium), thin or narrow materials are not suited to the process because the heat can cause them to distort.

This sort of cutting can be undertaken either manually or as an automated process. In the manual operation, the familiar worker in overalls, with full-face protection, provides the traditional image that sums up this process. In this scenario, the worker may often be welding, rather than cutting, materials.

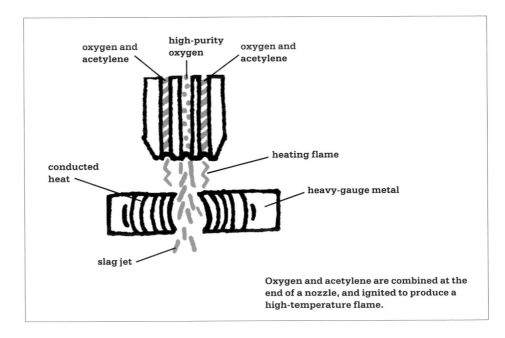

Oxygen and acetylene are combined at the end of a nozzle, and ignited to produce a high-temperature flame.

### Volumes of production

Compared with the alternatives for cutting thick metals, thermal cutting is an economical process for small-batch production.

### Unit price vs capital investment

Unless a cutting template is introduced, the process does not require tooling. In an automated process, the information for the shape can be provided by CAD files. Both of these factors mean that costs are kept down.

### Speed

The speed is greatly affected by the type of material used and its thickness. The process may be carried out manually, or it can be highly automated, with multi-torch, computer-operated systems. Speeds can reach up to 3 metres per minute.

### Surface

Cutting can be controlled to produce different grades of surface depending on the cost-versus-edge quality – that is, longer cutting times equal better edge finish. The finish of the edge is also determined by the material, but generally plasma-arc cutting (see p.27) will give the best finish.

### Types/complexity of shape

The process is best suited to heavy-gauge materials. Metals of below 8 millimetres may distort as a result of the intense heat, as might narrow sections. As in all sheet-cutting operations, nesting one shape within another (as you would when cutting biscuits from dough) to optimise space in between shapes produces an economical use of the material. The cut is generally at 90 degrees to the plate. Other angles can also be achieved, although this is not as easy to set up for oxyacetylene cutting as it is for plasma cutting.

### Scale

Using handheld cutting tools there is no maximum size, while in the automated process part sizes are restricted to the size of the machinery.

### Tolerances

Depend on the thickness of the material but, as a rule of thumb, they vary between ±1.5 millimetres for 6–35 millimetre-thick materials.

### Relevant materials

Limited to ferrous metals and titanium.

### Typical products

Heavy construction, including shipbuilding and machine components.

### Similar methods

Electron-beam machining (EBM) (p.18), plasma-arc cutting (p.27), laser cutting (p.40) and water-jet cutting (p.36).

### Further information

www.aws.org
www.twi.org.uk
www.iiw-iis.org

- Suited to thick metal plate.
- Adaptable to hand or automated use.

- Restricted to a narrow range of materials.

# Sheet-Metal Forming

Making objects from sheet metal is one of the earliest methods of human production. The Egyptians, for instance, made soft precious metals, such as gold, into sheets, from which they cut sometimes highly intricate forms.

One of the most refined applications for sheet-metal forming can be found in the production of the common whistle. Falling under the generic heading of solid-state forming, the production of whistles is an industrial craft, a multi-stage process that is based on the conversion of a sheet material into a three-dimensional object by cutting, press forming (see metal cutting, p.51) and, finally, plating sheets of brass. However, this overly simplified description masks the fact that this is a highly precise method of industrial production that requires extremely high levels of tolerance to produce a whistles with the perfect pitch.

The basic geometry of a whistle's body consists of three parts: an underside, mouthpiece and top and side. The pieces of brass are stamped out to form the flat nets and are then pressed into shape using a male and female jig. These components are soldered together, polished and plated in nickel. The final simple step: a cork pea is pushed into the mouthpiece.

In any wind instrument, the sound is the result of air flowing at different rates over a very sharp edge, producing two vibrating columns of air. After 135 years, Acme Whistles, in Birmingham in the UK, has tailored this highly precise process into an art form, producing a reject rate of just 3 per cent for their whistles. Considering the potential for the slightest, sometimes invisible, imperfection to produce the wrong sound, this really is a feat of crafted industrial manufacturing.

| Product | Acme Thunderer whistle |
|---|---|
| Designer | Joseph Hudson |
| Materials | nickel-coated brass (image shows the brass before plating) |
| Manufacturer | Acme Whistles |
| Country | UK |
| Date | 1884 |

The Acme Thunderer is shown here in its pre-assembled state, and before it is nickel-plated. This shows how many formed components go into making the final product.

### Volumes of production

This is a semi-automated method, so it can be used for production runs of greatly varying lengths.

### Unit price vs capital investment

This varies greatly, depending on the set-up and the volume of production required. Jewellers can use simple tools requiring very little investment. By contrast, millions of pounds would be needed to set up a production process for the whistle (pictured).

### Speed

Varies according to set-up. The Acme Thunderer featured here takes up to three days to produce.

### Surface

Generally, this is dependent on the finish of the sheet material, though polishing and painting are often required.

### Types/complexity of shape

The nature of this type of set-up allows jigs to be built to accommodate a range of quite complex shapes.

### Scale

There is no maximum size for sheet forming.

### Tolerances

Can be extremely high. In order to achieve perfect pitch in the whistle, tolerances are ± 0.0084 millimetres.

### Relevant materials

Soft metals such as brass, copper and aluminium are particularly easy to form, but any sheet metal can be used.

### Typical products

Sheet-metal forming is used to produce a number of products in a variety of industries – they range from brass musical instruments to computer housings and car bodies.

### Similar methods

Other processes that give form to flat sheets of metal include metal spinning (p.48), stamping and punching (see metal cutting, p.51), water-jet cutting (p.36), laser cutting (p.40) and CNC folding, a process in which sheet material, usually metal, is folded into different shapes – think of a biscuit tin.

### Further information

www.acmewhistles.co.uk

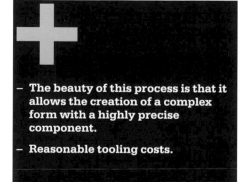

- **The beauty of this process is that it allows the creation of a complex form with a highly precise component.**
- **Reasonable tooling costs.**

- **Limited to sheet materials.**
- **The product may have to go through a number of stages.**

# Slumping Glass

To slump glass is to allow it to sink into shape. Most people know that if a sheet of glass is left alone long enough, its shape will slowly distort. However, glass does need to be heated to a sufficiently high temperature for it to reach an elastic state that enables it to move at an economical rate or, at the very least, faster than the hundreds of years it would take without heat. When a sheet of stiff glass is placed over a refractory mould (a mould made from a heat-resistant material) in a kiln and heated to 630°C, the glass relaxes enough to allow it to sag into a shape that becomes permanent once cooled.

To form the Fiam table (pictured), a blank sheet of 12-millimetre crystal glass is first cut. The computer-controlled process employs a jet of water, mixed with an abrasive powder, that passes at 1,000 metres per second through a tiny nozzle. This creates a jet strong enough to cut through any material. Once the flat blanks have been cut, the sheet is ready for curving.

The entire sheet and the refractory mould must be brought to the same critical melting temperature – even the smallest temperature variation can result in a broken sheet. At the right temperature, the glass is relaxed enough to sag under its own weight and sink into the mould, with a bit of manual assistance. The apparent simplicity of Fiam's products conceals the complex heating process, which has to be tightly regulated to keep the glass at exactly the right temperature inside the curving chamber. The pieces may be based on simple ideas and shapes, but this simplicity is only achieved (with a high success rate) by the use of sophisticated modern technology.

| Product | Toki side table |
|---|---|
| Designer | Setsu and Shinobu Ito |
| Materials | float glass |
| Manufacturer | Fiam Italia |
| Country | Italy |
| Date | 1995 |

The full radius of the table top curve, and the gentle curves of the feet, offer a suggestion of the simple forms that are possible with glass slumping.

### Volumes of production

Slumping is the kind of process that is as well suited to one-offs as it is to batch production.

### Unit price vs capital investment

Most commercially available moulds are made of either vitreous clay or stainless steel, but it is also possible to use plaster, cement or even found objects for low-volume production. Depending on the complexity of the shape, the process can involve a high failure rate of finished pieces and, therefore, high unit costs.

### Speed

Although this is an industrial process, the speed of forming is quite slow and still requires a considerable use of manual labour.

### Surface

Completely smooth glass surfaces can be achieved, as well as textures that can be incorporated into the mould.

### Types/complexity of shape

This process works on gravity, so any shape that is formed from a flat sheet and has a vertical drape is possible to achieve.

### Scale

Restricted only by the dimensions of the glass sheet and the kiln that provides the heat.

### Tolerances

Due to the difficulty of making glass slump into tight corners, coupled with the expansion of the glass, it can be difficult to achieve tight tolerances.

### Relevant materials

Most types of sheet glass (including borosilicate), soda-lime glass and advanced materials such as fused quartz and glass ceramic.

### Typical products

Domestic products such as bowls, plates, magazine racks, tables, chairs and tableware. Industrial applications include automotive windscreens, lighting reflectors, furnaces and fireplace windows.

### Similar methods

Draping glass over a mould, rather than into a mould, is also a valid process, and is sometimes just called 'draping'.

### Further information

www.fiamitalia.it
www.rayotek.com
www.sunglass.it

– Allows sheet glass to be formed into a unique three-dimensional shape in as little as a single operation.

– Slow, and a high degree of skill and experience can be required to trial and error a design.

# Metal Spinning
## including sheer and flow forming

Spinning is a widely used technique for bending sheet metal. As the name suggests, the process involves a flat metal disc, known as the blank, being spun, pushed and consequently wrapped around a rotating mandrel to produce curved, thin-walled shapes.

A flat metal sheet (the blank) is first clamped against the mandrel and then both are rotated at high speed, in the same direction. The spinning metal is then pushed with a tool – which in hand spinning is sometimes called the 'spoon' – against a wooden mandrel

| Product | Grito lampshade |
|---|---|
| Designer | El Ultimo Grito |
| Materials | aluminium with an anodised exterior and a powder-coated interior |
| Manufacturer | Mathmos |
| Country | UK |
| Date | 2003 |

There are thousands of products that are made using metal spinning, but what stands out with this 'spun' light is the additional process of laser cutting that has been used to create the sexy cut-away section of the lampshade, revealing a cross-section of a metal spinning not normally seen.

### Volumes of production

From single prototypes to batch production and runs of several thousand.

### Unit price vs capital investment

The tools for pushing and the mandrels are made from wood or metal, depending on the size of the component and the quantity required. For a small number of units it makes sense to use affordable wooden mandrels, but for large production runs metal is a better choice because the former will be subject to greater wear.

### Speed

Production cycle times are higher than for press forming (see metal cutting, p.51), but set-up times are substantially shorter, making metal spinning suitable for prototyping, one-offs and short- to medium-batch production.

### Surface

A spun surface may need to be polished in order to eliminate the circular witness lines on the external surface of the part.

### Types/complexity of shape

This is really only a technique for making symmetrical shapes that start with a sheet of metal. Discs, cones, hemispheres, cylinders and rings are the typical shapes made using this process. Undercuts and re-entrant angles are achieved by a split mandrel, which comes apart like the segments of an orange in order for the part to be released. Closed shapes such as hollow spheres are made by joining two halves together.

### Scale

Spun-metal products can be produced at less than 10 millimetres in diameter, and, at the other end of the scale, Acme Metal Spinning in the US has produced a shape that measures almost 3.5 metres across.

### Tolerances

Because the metal is stretched around the mandrel, the thickness of a part changes during the spinning process. The flatter the shape, the less the metal will need to stretch.

### Relevant materials

Spinning can be applied to a variety of metals, ranging from soft, ductile coppers and aluminium (which are the most common) to hard stainless steels.

### Typical products

The kitchen wok is a good example of an item made by spinning – it is even possible to see the evidence of its production in the concentric lines on the outside surface. Other products include bases and lampshades for lighting, cocktail shakers, urns and a whole mass of industrial components.

### Similar methods

Spinning is often combined with other techniques to produce more complex products. For example, pressure-formed parts are often spun to create necks, flanges and flares. Although far less common than spinning, incremental sheet forming (p.229) is a new process that allows a range of complex forms to be created from sheet metal using a single tool.

### Further information

www.centurymetalspinning.com
www.acmemetalspinning.com
www.metalforming.com
www.metal-spinners.co.uk

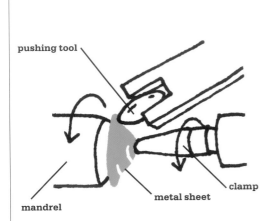

pushing tool

clamp

metal sheet

mandrel

A flat metal sheet is clamped against a mandrel and both are rotated at high speed. The metal is pushed with a tool until it conforms exactly to the mandrel's shape.

until it fits to the mandrel's shape. The resulting part is thus a copy of the external shape of this mandrel. Several operations can be performed in one set-up, and work pieces may have re-entrant profiles (undercuts). The design profile in relation to the centre line is therefore virtually unrestricted, though it will be symmetrical.

Sheer and flow forming are advanced forms of spinning that can be used to deliberately alter the wall thickness of metal parts by anything up to 75 per cent. It is ideal for concave, conical and convex hollow parts.

– Spinning is a very flexible form of mass-production, which can also lend itself to small-batch production.

– Low tooling costs.

– Can generate complex shapes without additional material removal (cutting) or joining processes.

– Some materials will harden in the spinning process.

– Spinning often requires post finishing.

– The process offers limited control over wall thickness because of the way the metal is slightly stretched over the mould.

# Metal Cutting
## including press forming, shearing, blanking, punching, bending, perforating, nibbling and stamping

In the metal industry the term 'cutting' is hardly ever used, because technically it is such a broad term it has almost no meaning. Cutting processes can be divided into two main categories: chip-forming and non-chip-forming. Press forming, shearing, blanking, punching, bending, perforating, nibbling and stamping are all terms that in one way or another describe non-chip-forming of metal sheet. Methods such as milling (see machining, p.12) and turning on a lathe (see p.20), on the other hand, are chip-forming techniques.

Punching and blanking are very similar in the sense that they both involve the removal of part of a sheet to form a hole. The processes differ in that punching is used to make sheets with shapes cut out of them, while blanking is a process for making separate shapes, similar to using a biscuit cutter to make many biscuits from rolled-out dough. The metal disc, which is the starting point for the beverage can tops (pictured), would have been made using blanking.

Nibbling is used to cut a sheet in successive bites from a small punch that pulses up and down in a process similar to that of a sewing-machine. Shearing involves a punch and a die with a tight control over the gap between the two (unlike punching, which doesn't have a die). The terms 'perforating' and 'bending' should be fairly self-explanatory.

| Product | beverage can ring-pull |
| --- | --- |
| Materials | aluminium |
| Manufacturer | Roxam |
| Country | UK |

This is an everyday product that has to be super cost-effective, yet must work all the time and must absolutely never cut your lip when you drink from it. Press forming and shearing are just two of the methods used to make this ubiquitous product.

Metal stamping is a cold forming process that is used to produce shallow components from metal sheet. Although it is a fairly straightforward method of cutting and forming sheet, it includes several variations, all of which combine a punching process together with a forming process, performed either in a sequence or in one action. A single die is needed for each operation, but the component can be removed and placed in another die for additional forming. Progressive dies (like a series of dies) are used in more complex procedures to form multiple actions.

### Volumes of production
The process can be used for manual production or for an automated CNC high-volume production.

### Unit price vs capital investment
Tooling costs can be reduced, or eliminated, by the use of existing punches or cutters, allowing for high-volume production to be achieved with low capital costs.

### Speed
Varies greatly, but typically 1500 drinks-can ring-pulls can be produced per minute.

### Surface
In terms of finishing, these cutting techniques will generally need deburring.

### Types/complexity of shape
Mostly used in the production of small components, and thickness is restricted to available standard sheet.

### Scale
Restricted by the standard sheet dimensions.

### Tolerances
High tolerances are achievable.

### Relevant materials
Restricted to sheet metal.

### Typical products
Cooling fan blades for electronics, washers, keyholes and watch components.

### Similar methods
Laser cutting (p.40) and water-jet cutting (p.36) are two non-chip-forming methods that can be set up to produce designs from CNC programs, without tooling costs.

### Further information
www.pma.org
www.nims-skills.org
www.khake.com/page88.html

- Very versatile in terms of producing different shapes.
- Can be used for any solid metal.
- High degree of accuracy.

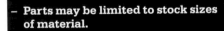

- Parts may be limited to stock sizes of material.
- Material utilisation can be low due to wastage.

# Thermoforming
## including vacuum, pressure, drape and plug-assisted forming

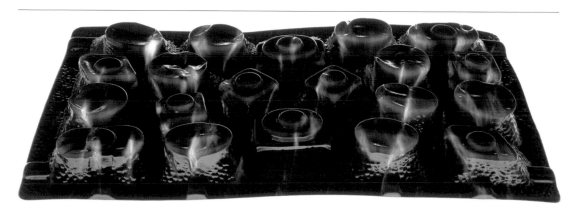

Thermoforming is one of the most common methods of producing plastic components and any art student who has been through the traditional foundation course will have used a vacuum-forming machine. Vacuum forming is one of the few plastic-forming methods that is as accessible to school and college students as it is to large-scale industrial production. It is also one the easiest methods of production to comprehend, and if you have ever seen the process in operation you will understand why.

The basic materials needed for this process are a thermoplastic sheet and a former. Because the pressures employed are low, the former can be made of wood, aluminium or other fairly inexpensive materials. The former is the exact shape of the part required and is placed at the centre of a table, which can be raised and dropped. The rigid plastic sheet is heated under a series of convection bars similar to a domestic oven, until the plastic is soft, pliable and saggy. At this point, the former is raised on its

| Product | chocolate-box tray |
|---|---|
| Materials | Plantic biodegradable polymer |
| Date | 2005 |

There are few better examples of thermoforming than a chocolate-box tray. The individual shapes of the chocolates are evidence of the shape of the mould that is used to form the trays.

1  The former (in this case a simple wooden shape for a college project) is placed on the bed.

2  Once the bed has been lowered, the plastic sheet is placed on top, ready to be clamped by the metal frame.

3  The heater is lowered onto the plastic sheet.

4  A vacuum is applied to form the shape.

bed, pushing into the soft sheet, and a vacuum is applied. This sucks the air out from below and pulls the plastic onto the former. Once the plastic has 'hugged' the former and cooled slightly, it can be removed for post finishing.

Other forms of thermoforming include pressure forming, which works in the opposite way to vacuum forming by forcing the material into the mould. Drape forming, as the name suggests, consists of draping a sheet of heated plastic over a male mould, where it is mechanically stretched allowing the sheet to remain close to its original thickness. Plug-assisted forming uses plugs to pre-stretch the plastic before the vacuum is introduced. Again, this allows for greater control over the material thickness.

# Vacuum forming

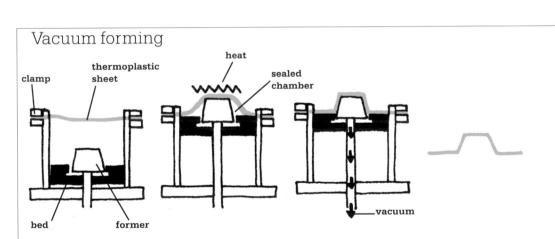

1  The former is placed onto a bed and lowered into a chamber.

2  Here, it is covered by the thermoplastic sheet, which is clamped into a metal frame, creating a sealed chamber.

3  The plastic sheet is heated from above until it becomes flexible. The former is then raised and a pump is activated, resulting in air being drawn from the chamber and the sheet being sucked over the mould.

4  Once the plastic has 'hugged' the former and cooled slightly, it is removed for finishing.

### Volumes of production

Suitable for model makers' prototype work and one-offs, but also for large-scale production.

### Unit price vs capital investment

Formers can be made from a range of materials, depending on the number of components that is required. The ease of machining and its wear-resistance makes aluminium suitable for large production runs. Epoxy resins are used as a cheap alternative to aluminium, but anything can really be used, including MDF, plaster, wood and even plasticine, which is actually excellent for vacuum forming shapes with undercuts, because you can pick it out afterwards.

### Speed

Bathtubs can be made at a rate of one every five minutes. Beyond this, speed is difficult to estimate, because multi-mould formers can rapidly speed up the process, and, besides this, the thickness of the material affects the time it takes to heat up sufficiently.

### Surface

Vacuum forming picks up surface details very well, so the surface finish of the mould is reflected in the surface finish on the part.

### Types/complexity of shape

You will need draft angles, because undercuts are impossible to achieve with standard tooling.

### Scale

A 2 by 2-metre aperture is standard, but it can be even bigger.

### Tolerances

Varies, depending on size of the formed piece. As a guide, a forming of less than 150 millimetres will hold a tolerance of 0.38 millimetres.

### Relevant materials

Most thermoplastics that are supplied as sheets. Typical examples include polystyrene, ABS (acrylonitrile butadiene styrene), acrylics and polycarbonates.

### Typical products

Canoes, bathtubs, packaging, furniture, interior car trim and shower trays.

### Similar methods

Superforming aluminium (p.56) and inflating metal (p.62).

### Further information

www.formech.com
www.thermoformingdivision.com
www.bpf.co.uk/bpfindustry/process_
   plastics_thermoforming.cfm
www.rpc-group.com

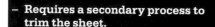

**+**

- **Equally suitable for small or large production runs.**

- **Low pressure, so tooling can be fairly cheap.**

- **Suitable for in-mould decoration.**

- **Multiple parts can be made using a single multi-former.**

**−**

- **Requires a secondary process to trim the sheet.**

- **No vertical sides on the finished part; draft angles are a must.**

- **Can have undercuts, but these need special tooling.**

# Superforming Aluminium
## including cavity, bubble, back-pressure and diaphragm forming

The process of heating a sheet of plastic, draping it over a mould and sucking the air out has been in use for some time (see thermoforming, p.53). However, as the speed of the development of new materials increases, more technologies overlap when it comes to both materials and processes. Superforming involves such an overlap, since it brings traditional vacuum forming with plastic to aluminium alloys. The process is achieved through four main methods: cavity forming, bubble forming, back-pressure forming and diaphragm forming, each suited to specific applications. The common element in all these methods is the

### Cavity forming

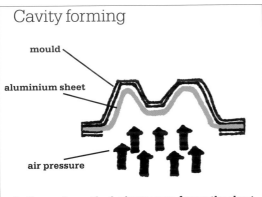

In the cavity method, air pressure forces the sheet up into the tool.

### Bubble forming

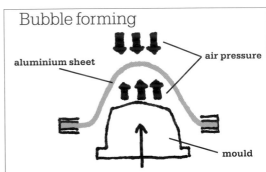

Air pressure blows the sheet into a bubble. A mould is then pushed up into the bubble and air pressure is applied from the top, forcing the material to conform to the shape of the mould.

### Back-pressure forming

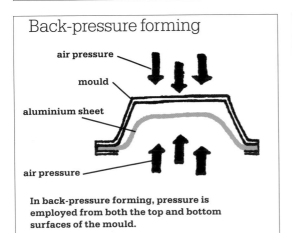

In back-pressure forming, pressure is employed from both the top and bottom surfaces of the mould.

### Diaphragm forming

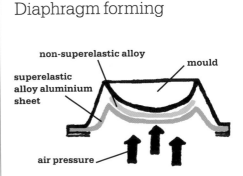

Air pressure forces the heated superelastic aluminium onto a heated non-superelastic alloy which is then formed over the mould.

heating of an aluminium sheet to 450–500°C in a pressurised forming oven, and then forcing it over, or into, a single surface tool to create a complex three-dimensional shape.

In the cavity method, air pressure forces the sheet up into the tool in a process that can be described as 'reverse vacuum forming'. According to the manufacturers, this process is ideal for forming large, complex parts such as automotive body panels.

In bubble forming, the air pressure forces the material into a bubble. A mould is then pushed up into the bubble and air pressure is applied from the top, forcing the material to conform to the shape of the mould. Bubble forming is suitable for deep and relatively complex mouldings that are difficult to achieve with the other superforming processes.

Back-pressure forming uses pressure from both the top and bottom surfaces of the mould to maintain the integrity of the sheet and allow for the forming of difficult alloys.

Diaphragm forming is a process that allows for 'non-superelastic' alloys to be formed. The non-superelastic material is 'hugged' over the mould using a combination of a sheet of heated 'superelastic' aluminium and air pressure.

| Product | MN01 bike |
| --- | --- |
| Designers | Marc Newson & Toby Louis-Jensen |
| Materials | aluminium |
| Manufacturer | Superform Aluminium |
| Country | UK |
| Date | 1999 |

This bike is a good example of the transfer of industrial manufacturing processes into consumer products by experimental projects. The text embossed onto the frame also illustrates the detail that is achievable.

### Volumes of production

At present, production runs of about 1,000 parts are considered large, but mass-production is a possibility, with some carmakers starting to use the process on a larger scale.

### Unit price vs capital investment

High capital investment, mainly in tooling and material, but the costs per unit are reduced as the volume of production increases.

### Speed

Depends on the material – some alloys can be formed in three to four minutes, while the structural alloys used in aircraft, for example, may need up to an hour to form.

### Surface

Excellent surface quality.

### Types/complexity of shape

This depends on the specific method you use. Bubble forming allows the greatest degree of complexity in shape, but with all methods the basic principle is about creating three-dimensional shapes from a flat sheet. Draft angles need to be considered in order for parts to be removed from the mould. Undercuts are not recommended.

### Scale

Each method is suited to different scales and thicknesses of material, for example, using back-pressure forming, parts can be made up to approximately 4.5 metres square. Cavity forming can only process smaller sheet sizes, although these can be up to 10 millimetres thick.

### Tolerances

Typically ±1 millimetre for larger parts.

### Relevant materials

This process is specifically designed for use with what are known as 'superelastic' types of aluminium. However, the diaphragm-forming method enables the processing of non-superelastic materials.

### Typical products

A large market for this process is in the aerospace and automotive industries. Designers such as Ron Arad and Marc Newson have applied it to diverse furniture and bicycles. On the London Underground, architect Norman Foster used superforming to produce tunnel-cladding panels for Southwark station.

### Similar methods

For plastic, vacuum forming (p.53), for glass, slumping (p.46), and for metal, look at the inflated stainless steel by Stephen Newby (p.62).

### Further information

www.superform-aluminium.com

---

**+**

- Complex forms can be created within a single component.
- A range of sheet thicknesses can be used.
- Can create subtle details and forms, without spring-back issues.

**—**

- Limited to aluminium alloys.

# Explosive Forming
## AKA High-Energy-Rate Forming

Can you imagine the fun in discovering this process? In a way it reminds me of the TV-show character Mr Bean, who decided to paint his living room by planting an explosive in a tin of paint. However unlikely, explosive forming is actually an established method of forming metal sheet or tube. It is also another great example of a process that demonstrates the lateral thinking used by engineers to pursue new methods of making things.

The first use of explosive forming was documented in 1888, when it was employed in the forming of plate engravings. The First and Second World Wars provided an intense period of development, as a result of which explosive forming became a major

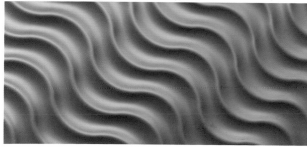

| Product | Desert Storm architectural panels |
| --- | --- |
| Materials | coil-coated aluminium |
| Manufacturer | Exploform |
| Country | Germany |
| Date | Exploform BV created 1998 |

These architectural panels show the scale of panels and the complex patterns that can be achieved with explosive forming.

process for manufacturing missile nose cones in the 1950s. Today, explosive forming exists in two forms – 'standoff', where the explosive is positioned at a distance from the metal, either in the open air or submersed in water or oil, and 'contact forming', where the explosive is in direct contact with the metal.

In simple terms, the sheet or tube is placed in a vacuum-sealed die cavity, which is in turn placed under water (unless it is the open-air method). A charge is placed over the sheet and detonated, sending shockwaves through the water and rapidly forcing the material into the die cavity.

### Volumes of production

Explosive forming can be used for one-off art projects such as sculptures and installations, but it is equally suitable for mass-production of industrial components. In former East Germany it was used to make hundreds of thousands of cardan axles for heavy trucks.

### Unit price vs capital investment

If conventional pressing or spinning can be used, they would usually be cheaper, but relatively low tooling costs and the ability to manufacture complex shapes can make explosive forming the best option available.

### Speed

Varies enormously depending on the size and complexity of the shape. Sometimes it is possible to manufacture twenty small parts in one explosion, while larger, more intricate shapes can require up to six explosions over three days. Even a single explosion is quite time-consuming, however, due to the lengthy set-up time (amounting to over an hour per explosion).

### Surface

Surface quality is generally extremely good. It is possible to form grade 2G (chemically polished) stainless steel without damaging even the protective foil, producing parts with a perfect mirror finish.

### Types/complexity of shape

Ideal for forming complex shapes with seamless cavities.

### Scale

Specific manufacturers can form sheets of nickel up to an incredible thickness of 13 millimetres, with lengths of up to 10 metres. Larger sheets are only achievable by welding sheets together.

### Tolerances

Able to maintain precise tolerances.

### Relevant materials

The process is not restricted to soft metals such as aluminium, but embraces all metals, including titanium, iron and nickel alloys.

### Typical products

Large architectural components and panels, and parts for the aerospace and automotive industries.

### Similar methods

Superforming aluminium (p.56) and inflating metal (p.62).

### Further information

www.exploform.com

Although this image does not show the close-up workings of the process, it does give some indication of the scale and the sealed, pressurised environment in which the explosive forming takes place.

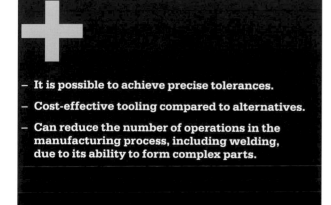

- It is possible to achieve precise tolerances.
- Cost-effective tooling compared to alternatives.
- Can reduce the number of operations in the manufacturing process, including welding, due to its ability to form complex parts.

- Limited number of manufacturers.
- Must adhere to strict safety regulations.

# Inflating Metal

From its extraction when creating vacuums to its sudden introduction into a pre-form to create plastic bottles, air is often a key material in production methods. In terms of blow forming, it is thousands of years old, and its earliest use was in the forming of glass. British designer Stephen Newby, however, has recently introduced a way of inflating stainless steel sheet to create new possibilities in visual language for this hard metal.

The soft appearance of the inflated shapes contrasts with the tough, hard quality of the steel. The process (which, at the time of writing, has a patent pending) literally involves inflating two sheets of metal that have been sandwiched together and sealed at the edges, without using moulds. Each inflated piece, therefore, responds in a different way, producing a unique piece. In terms of size, the pieces are only limited by the original sheet size. A variety of textured and coloured stainless steels can be used – these are not damaged in the process because the metal is formed from the inside.

| Product | inflated stainless steel pillows |
|---|---|
| Designer | Stephen Newby |
| Materials | stainless steel |
| Manufacturer | Full Blown Metals |
| Country | UK |
| Date | 2002 |

The indentations in these pillow shapes are the natural result of the metal creasing when it is inflated from the two sheets of steel that are sandwiched together.

**Volumes of production**
Best suited to batch production.

**Unit price vs capital investment**
No tooling, but some designs require prototyping.

**Speed**
Blow forming (of which inflating metal is just one example) is instantaneous. The process is semi-automated and runs at different times according to size. For example, an inflated 10-centimetre metal square can be produced at the rate of 30 squares per hour.

**Surface**
Full range of high-quality factory-applied finishes, including mirror finishes, colours, etchings, textures and embossed finishes.

**Types/complexity of shape**
Any shape that can be produced from flat two-dimensional templates, including organic forms, figurative lettering, soft, cushion-like creased forms and smooth, uncreased forms.

**Scale**
From 5 centimetres up to the maximum single sheet size, typically 3 by 2 metres.

**Tolerances**
5 millimetres per 1,000 millimetres in overall dimensions.

**Relevant materials**
Most metals including stainless steel, mild steel, aluminium, brass and copper.

**Typical products**
Architectural cladding and screens, large-scale public art, outdoor design, including water features, and contemporary interior products.

**Similar methods**
Glass blowing by hand (p.98) and superforming aluminium (p.56).

**Further information**
www.fullblownmetals.com

- Ability to form unique shapes in metal.

- High strength-to-weight ratio.

- The process can be used to form high-tensile strength materials.

- Factory-applied finishes are preserved in the forming process.

- Specific dimensions are easily achieved without the need for moulds or jigs.

- Offered only by a single manufacturer.

# Bending Plywood

The conversion of a tree into a simple-looking piece of bent plywood furniture involves at least 35 steps. The technique of cross-laminating veneers to produce stable, stiff engineered materials was first understood by the ancient Egyptians, who used the process for making items such as their iconic sarcophagi. The development of modern bent plywood is the result of a range of technological advancements, including the ability to cut the veneers accurately, the presses to laminate them and the glues to construct them.

The processing of most natural materials tends to be concentrated in the locations where the materials originate, and plywood production takes place mainly in northern Europe, North America, Southeast Asia and Japan. Starting from the point where the veneers have been sliced or rotary-cut from the logs, these large strips are cut into individual sheets, which are subsequently dried by being passed through a long chamber, at the end of which they are stacked according to quality.

The veneers are fed into rollers that distribute an even layer of glue over each sheet, with the quantity of glue being determined by the porosity of the timber. The various sheets are then stacked, with the grain running in alternate directions, to form an odd number of layers. The assembled sheets are placed over the female part of a mould, with the male part clamped on

| Product | **Elica Folding Chair** |
|---|---|
| Designer | Gudmunder Ludvik |
| Materials | plywood and sandblasted steel leg supports |
| Manufacturer | Lapalma |
| Country | Italy |
| Date | 2005 |

The thin, elegant frame for this folding chair demonstrates that strength can be achieved even with a material as thin as plywood.

top. The moulds allow for an excess of veneers, which is trimmed to form neat edges once the glue has dried. Depending on the shape, a pressure of several tonnes is needed to compact the sandwich together. The vertical pressure is aided by horizontal pressure, forcing the moulds to come together from all sides, and a combination of heat and pressure cure the glue. The part stays in the mould for about 25 minutes, the exact time depending on the shape. In industrial production, a CNC (computer numerical controlled) cutter is then used to trim the uneven layers to form a clean edge.

## Volumes of production

Jigs can be made up for single profiles in a small workshop. Industrial production set-ups can produce hundreds of thousands of units.

## Unit price vs capital investment

Jigs for low-volume production can be expensive due to the labour costs involved. However, depending on the design, simple moulds can be made that are still economical for small production runs or even one-offs. At the industrial end of the scale, as with most other manufacturing processes, higher tooling costs are balanced by low unit costs.

## Speed

Cycle times are fairly long because the glued veneers have to dry inside the mould before they can be taken out, and the parts need subsequent finishing, including edge trimming, surface treatments or painting.

## Surface

Dependent on the type of wood.

## Types/complexity of shape

Restricted to simple bends in a single direction. The inherent flexibility of the material can allow for slight undercuts when removing pieces from the moulds.

## Scale

The scale is generally suited to furniture and accessories (such as magazine racks). The restriction on size is determined by the size of the moulds and the ability to exert the degree of pressure needed to compact the layers.

## Tolerances

Rather low because of the flexibility of the material.

## Relevant materials

Birch is used in the majority of mass-produced furniture, but many other types of timber, including oak and maple, can be used. Burly woods (the outgrowth of a tree, also known as the burr), including pine, are not to be recommended, because it is difficult to produce plywood of consistent quality from them.

## Typical products

Furniture, interiors and architectural cladding. Aircraft frames were made from bent plywood during the two World Wars.

## Similar methods

Inflating wood (p.166) and pressing plywood (p.70).

## Further information

www.woodweb.com
www.woodforgood.com
www.artek.fi
www.vitra.com
www.hermanmiller.com

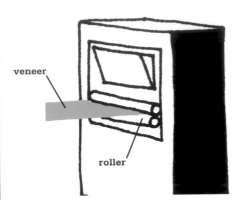

veneer

roller

1  The veneers are fed into rollers, which distribute an even layer of glue to each sheet.

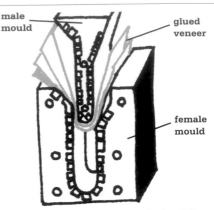

male mould

glued veneer

female mould

2  The veneers are stacked and the assembled sheets are placed over a female mould and the male part clamped tightly on top. The moulds allow for an excess of veneers, which will be trimmed once the glue has dried.

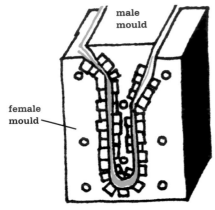

male mould

female mould

3  Pressure is applied to compact the sandwich together. The vertical pressure is aided by horizontal pressure, forcing the moulds together from all sides.

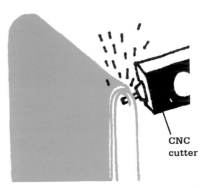

CNC cutter

4  Once cured, the part is removed and trimmed to form a clean edge.

+

– Can accommodate a range of thicknesses.
– Allows for strong, lightweight components.

–

– Involves many steps.
– Restricted to bends in a single direction.

# Deep Three-Dimensional Forming in Plywood

This book features a number of new and radical ways to process plywood into ever more complicated and curved forms. One of these is deep three-dimensional forming in plywood, a combination of a production method and a material specifically developed for the purpose. Using an innovative treatment in which the wood fibres are relaxed, it is now possible to bend plywood into wavy shapes that were once unthinkable.

The technology for preparing the plywood was developed by the German manufacturer Reholz®, and it enables the plywood to be moulded into a deep, three-dimensional compound curve, which is capable of producing forms that resemble moulded plastic rather than a piece of wood.

The key to this process, and the first stage in achieving the complex curves, is a series of closely cut, parallel lines, so deeply cut into the individual veneers that the wood itself almost falls apart. This gives the veneers the elasticity to be bent in different directions without breaking, which is particularly important when bending them against the direction of the grain. The individual sheets of veneer are glued together in a way that is similar to the bent wood process (see p.64), in order to achieve stiffness and strength.

| Product | Gubi chair |
|---|---|
| Designer | Komplot |
| Materials | Walnut veneer |
| Manufacturer | Gubi using Reholz® deep-3D forming technology |
| Country | Germany (process) Denmark (chair) |
| Date | 2003 |

The apparently simple curves of the Gubi chair mask the sophistication of this completely new method of forming wood. The compound curves (the seat passes through an almost 90 degree angle) are a result of the ability of this treated ply to conform to far more complex shapes than, for example, the pressed plywood tray (see p.70).

## Volumes of production
Suitable for mass-production.

## Unit price vs capital investment
The process is not cheap, but it is the only way to achieve this level of freedom in shaping plywood, which can go a long way in justifying the investment in tooling for large production runs.

## Speed
The Reholz® process involves several steps, including the pre-treatment of the veneer, pressing and, finally, trimming. The real difference, however, between standard bent plywood manufacturing (see p.64) and the deep three-dimensional forming process is just one step – the cutting treatment to which the basic veneers are subjected that enables the plywood to be bent.

## Surface
Comparable to any other type of close-grained wood surface, which can be stained, painted and coated in a number of ways.

## Types/complexity of shape
The key here is that deep three-dimensional forming allows layers of thin, prepared veneer to be built up into formed sheets of plywood capable of being bent into previously unachievable curves. Designs should allow for the component to be separated from male and female moulds, so there can be no undercuts.

## Scale
The scale is limited by the size of the veneers available and the moulds used to form the final shape.

## Tolerances
Because of natural variations in the grain of the wood, no moulding is exactly like any other and it can be difficult to achieve very high tolerances. This can, nevertheless, be dealt with in a number of ways, for instance by using flexible fixings.

## Relevant materials
Although many basic veneers can be used for deep three-dimensional forming, it is important that the veneer should have a straight grain direction and no knots. High-quality ALPI-veneers are especially suitable (these, recommended by Reholz® who developed the technology, are veneers produced by the Italian company, ALPI).

## Typical products
Chair seats, plywood bars, bent furniture frames or, on a larger scale, laminated wood structures for use in the construction industry. Deep three-dimensional formed plywood can also be used to coat the housings of medical devices, for example, panelling for MRI (magnetic resonance imaging) scanning machines and in packaging to replace MDF (medium density fibreboard), mouldings for lights and parts of automobile interiors.

## Similar methods
The manufacturer compares this process to the deep-drawing of metal sheets. However, in terms of wood production the closest method is bending plywood (p.64), although this has the disadvantage of being formable in only a single direction. The inflated wood process (p.166) developed by Malcolm Jordan allows similar three-dimensional forms to be produced, but it requires both foam and plywood. Pressing plywood (p.70), which is used to make dinner trays and car dashboards, achieves a similar three-dimensional effect, but with much shallower results.

## Further information
www.reholz.de

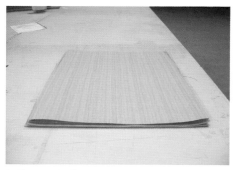

1 The stack of prepared sheets of veneer assembled with the grain running in alternate directions.

2 The stack of veneers before the male and female moulds are brought together.

3 The seat for the Gubi chair, post forming.

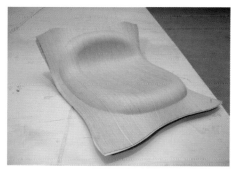

4 The seat is ready for the final shaping process, which involves the excess material around the seat being cut away.

- Permits new forms to be produced from plywood.

- Allows wood to enter markets normally reserved for metals and plastics.

- Enhances the structural strength of plywood.

- There are some limitations with regard to small radii and other sharp bends.

- Since this is a wood process, mouldings will never be as accurate as, for example, plastic components.

- Available only from Reholz®, the originator of the technology.

# Pressing Plywood

The first noteworthy thing about this production method is that the products it is used for are formed by a method that is more reminiscent of plastic forming than wood forming. By that I mean that they are formed from a flat sheet of wood into a three-dimensional shape in a way that gives results similar to shallow plastic vacuum thermoforming (see p.53).

The first stage of the process for making the archetypal trays you find in canteens around the world involves the raw material of veneers being cut and trimmed into square sheets. In most cases a single layer of veneer will be made up of two narrow leaves which are 'sewn' together with a flat, cross-hatched thread of glue. The

sheets are stacked together and arranged with the grain running in alternate directions and with sheets of glue-impregnated paper in between each sheet. A melamine-impregnated sheet is added to the top and bottom of this stack, like the bread in a sandwich. The sandwiched packs are then placed in a press, in between male and female moulds, where pressure is applied for approximately four minutes at 135°C. It is important for the veneers to have a good degree of moisture to prevent the wood from splitting. Once removed from the press, the trays are stored on a flat table and held down with weights to ensure that they do not warp. The final stage involves the edges being

| Product | dinner tray |
|---|---|
| Designer | not applicable |
| Materials | lacquered birch |
| Manufacturer | Neville & Sons |
| Country | UK |

This sequence of images shows the layers of veneers and glue-impregnated paper; a pressed, untrimmed plywood tray; and the trimmed, lacquer-sealed tray.

trimmed and sealed with a spray of a clear lacquer.

The combination of heat, pressure and adhesive enables a range of laminated wood products to be produced, resulting in thin-section designs that can be extremely strong. Neville and Sons in the UK have been making an assortment of trays for several years. Today, they are one of the few remaining UK-based companies still producing wooden laminated trays. It is through the action of heat and pressure that they can make durable trays of only about 15 millimetres deep.

### Volumes of production

As many as 600 wooden trays can be produced in a day. Minimum orders from Neville and Sons are 50 units.

### Unit price vs capital investment

An affordable ratio for small-scale production makes this method of forming highly suitable for small- and large-scale runs. Moulds for trays are produced in aluminium covered in a stainless steel sheet, which makes them cost-effective even for batch production. Unit prices are very low.

### Speed

One tray can be produced every five minutes.

### Surface

The surface colour, and to a degree the finish and pattern, are controlled by the melamine sheet that is used in the pressing process. Decorative patterns, colours and non-slip surfaces are available.

### Types/complexity of shape

Embossed sheets with a fairly low-draw impression, up to a maximum of approximately 25 millimetres.

### Scale

Neville and Sons can produce products measuring up to 600 by 450 millimetres.

### Tolerances

Not applicable.

### Relevant materials

Most veneers are suitable. However, the material used for trays is generally birch, beech or mahogany.

### Typical products

Given the shallowness of the depth achievable, this process is limited to products such as trays and automotive trim with the kind of walnut effect you would expect to find in high-end brands.

### Similar methods

A process that allows for much more depth and possibilities with curving plywood is deep 3D forming (p.67). Also relevant, but using a completely different technology, is the inflated wood by Curvy Composites (p.166).

### Further information

www.nevilleuk.com

- Extremely durable: heat-resistant and dishwasher-safe.
- Excellent chemical resistance.
- Printable surface.

- Difficult to produce deep impressions.

# 3:
# Contin

# UOUS

## Components that are made from continuous lengths of a material

This chapter looks at components that are made according to the same principles that are used to make sausages, or, in other words, components that are the result of material being fed through a shape to produce long lengths of the same profile. It also looks at continuous strips of wood and plastic, woven lengths of metal and continuous lengths of bent steel. It celebrates a rich assortment of processes that use a range of dies to form materials that can be produced in infinitely long length but which, with one exception, have the same cross-sectional shape along the whole length. Many of these processes are extremely cost-effective because they can produce identical multiples, cut from the same strip or section.

# Calendering

Calendering has traditionally been used as a finishing process applied to textiles and paper, using heat and pressure to give a smooth, shiny surface. In the nineteenth century, however, it was developed so that multiple rollers could produce rubber sheet. It is a large-scale process, both in terms of the volumes it can produce and the sheer size of the machine that is used to form the sheet material itself (or to add texture to existing sheet materials).

Imagine a machine that has at its heart a series of steel rollers resembling a clothes mangle, that press materials into continuous lengths of thin sheet. Although still used for finishing paper, some forms of textiles and various types of elastics, calendering is the preferred method for forming high

volumes of PVC sheet at a fast rate. In the realm of plastic production it competes with extrusion (see p.78) in the production of both rigid and flexible plastic sheet.

When it is used in this sort of plastic production, the set-up usually includes at least four heated rollers, rotating at different speeds. Before this, however, hot granules of the plastic are fed into a kneader where they reach a gelling stage. They are then fed, via a conveyor belt, through the first of the heated rollers. The rollers are carefully controlled to produce the correct thickness and finish. Embossing rollers can be used to add texture and the sheet material then passes through cooling rollers prior to being wound onto a giant roll.

The essence of calendering is captured in this image, which shows a ribbon of plastic being passed over polished steel rollers to form a continuous length of plastic sheet.

### Volumes of production

Because of the set-up costs and running times involved, tooling is expensive, making calendering exclusively a very high-volume production process. The minimum length for production varies between 2,000 and 5,000 metres, depending on the gauge of the sheet.

### Unit price vs capital investment

Calendered sheets are often further converted in order to be turned into products, but the price of the sheet before it is converted is highly cost-effective if large enough orders are fulfilled. Capital investment is extremely high.

### Speed

Once the process is running at optimum speed – which can take several hours to achieve – it is super-fast.

### Surface

The rollers can be ultra-smooth to give a shiny surface, or embossed with patterns that are transferred onto the final sheet.

### Types/complexity of shape

Flat, thin sheet.

### Scale

The thickness of a PVC sheet is generally between 0.06 and 1.2 millimetres. The width of the rolls is up to 1,500 millimetres.

### Tolerances

Not applicable.

### Relevant materials

Calendering can be used for a range of materials, including textiles, composites, plastics (mainly PVC) or paper, where it is used to smooth the surface.

### Typical products

Paper, used for newsprint, and large-scale plastic sheet or film. It can also be used as a finishing process for other papers and textiles.

### Similar methods

In terms of plastic production, extrusion (p.78) is the closest comparable method for producing continuous sheet material. There is also blown film (p.76).

### Further information

www.vinyl.org
www.ecvm.org
www.ipaper.com
www.coruba.co.uk

- Produces long, continuous rolls without joins.

- Excellent method for producing large quantities of flat sheets.

- Suited to very large-scale production only.

# Blown Film

The best way to summarise the blown-film process is to think of blowing bubblegum, but on a giant industrial scale. Producing plastic that is on the physical scale of a building involves a massive tubular bubble of inflated plastic being blown upwards into a vertical scaffolding structure.

The technique takes its name from the action of the plastic granules, which are heated (1) and fed vertically by a stream of air through a horizontally placed cylindrical die (2), to form a thin-walled tube that is blown to form a huge plastic bubble (3). This bubble is fed vertically by

These two photographs convey the huge physical scale of this type of manufacturing as the bubble of plastic emerges from the die and the flattened tube descends through the rollers.

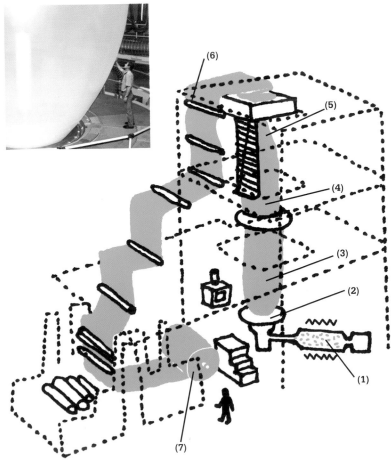

a stream of air in the top of the die to form a tower of plastic (4). Varying the volume of air in the bubble controls the thickness and width of the film, which gradually cools as it rises, tapers and, several metres up, eventually subsides completely into a flattened tube (5). This flat tube passes through a series of rollers on its way back down to ground level (6), where it is wound onto a giant roll, ready for despatch (7). The edges of this sheet material can be trimmed off to produce sheets, or it can be left as a tube to be used for supermarket bags and bin-liners.

### Volumes of production
This is a high-volume method with a capacity to convert 250 kilograms of plastic per hour.

### Unit price vs capital investment
High capital costs, but extremely cost-effective for large production runs.

### Speed
Up to 130 metres per minute.

### Surface
Controlled by various factors, including the material and machinery set-up.

### Types/complexity of shape
Flat sheets or tubes only.

### Scale
Blown films range from 660 millimetres to 5 metres in diameter, and can be up to hundreds of metres in length. Films are available in thicknesses of from 10 or 20 microns up to 250 microns.

### Tolerances
This process can achieve high tolerances, but you should be aware that some manufacturers offer two grades of blown film – with and without thickness control.

### Relevant materials
The most common materials are high- and low-density polyethylene, but other materials, such as polypropylene and nylon, can also be used.

### Typical products
Most plastic film products, such as bin-liners, carrier bags, sheeting, cling film, laminating film and just about any other type of film you care to mention.

### Similar methods
Extrusion (p.78) and calendering (p.74) are both used to produce thin flat sheets.

### Further information
www.plasticbag.com
www.flexpack.org
www.reifenhauser.com

**+**
– Allows for the production of a material with uniform properties across the whole length and width.

**—**
– Blown film is not always ideal – for example, the process of casting film can be a better option for applications that require high optical clarity.

# Extrusion

Extrusion occurs in a variety of forms, from the low-tech squeeze of a toothpaste tube and the making of foods such as long-stranded pasta, to aluminium window frames and the continuous lengths of hard-boiled egg that McDonald's slices into its salads. In the simplest terms, extrusion is about squeezing a material through a hole in a die and producing continuous lengths of material at whatever profile that hole has.

Tom Dixon has developed a slightly unconventional use for extrusions in his 'Fresh Fat' range of furniture and accessories. Developing his own tooling to manufacture the products, which are a combination of woven, knotted and tangled forms, Dixon relies on the fact that plastic in its soft and malleable state can do pretty much anything you want it to do. So, if you wanted (as he does) to squeeze a continuous narrow strip

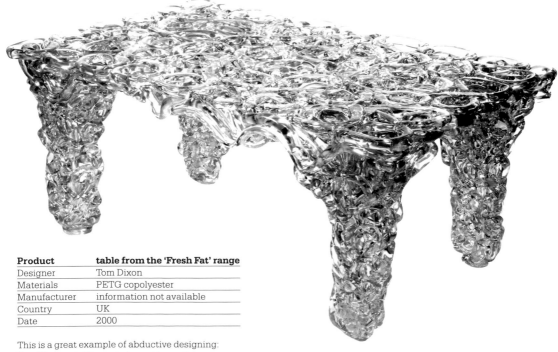

| Product | table from the 'Fresh Fat' range |
|---|---|
| Designer | Tom Dixon |
| Materials | PETG copolyester |
| Manufacturer | information not available |
| Country | UK |
| Date | 2000 |

This is a great example of abductive designing: Tom Dixon acts like a pirate seeking out new treasures from industry, in this case extruded copolyester, to turn into products.

## Volumes of production

Different manufacturers have different minimum lengths, but extrusion can be a cost-effective process for both batch and large-scale runs. It is definitely not for one-offs – unless your one-off is 50 metres long.

## Unit price vs capital investment

Conventional extrusion requires a low investment in tooling when compared with injection moulding (see p.178), for example. Tom Dixon's method requires only the moulds in which the 'spaghetti' is draped.

## Speed

Up to 20 metres per hour.

## Surface

Excellent.

## Types/complexity of shape

No problems in making complex shapes with varying wall thicknesses, just as long as the shape is the same along the whole length. Flat sheet can also be produced.

## Scale

Depends on the type of extrusion. Most manufacturers have an average maximum size of 250 millimetres in cross-section. The length is limited by the size of the factory.

## Tolerances

Difficult to maintain high tolerances due to a wearing of the die.

## Relevant materials

The 'Fresh Fat' range is made from a copolymer called Provista, developed by the Eastman Chemical Company. However, there are many other materials with low melting points that can be processed by extrusion, including wood-based plastic composites, aluminium, magnesium, copper and ceramics.

## Typical products

Everything from architectural and furniture components, lighting and accessories, to pasta, and sticks of rock candy with place names written through them.

## Similar methods

Pultrusion (p.81), calendering (p.74), coextrusion (multiple layers of extruded material in the same component), laminating (two, or more, materials bonded together), roll forming (p.86) and impact extrusion (p.128).

## Further information

www.eastman.com
www.tomdixon.net
www.aec.org

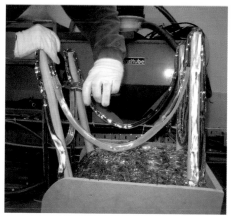

1 The hot, plastic 'spaghetti' is formed over a wooden mould.

2 A skilled craftsman forms the legs of this industrial craft product.

of plastic into a mould and let it drape and collect into a controlled mass, then that's exactly what it would do.

The products in this range, which includes chairs, a chaise longue and bowls, all express the principle of plastic moulding in its most basic form: plastic is always, at one stage, a hot goo that, when cooled, occupies the form that surrounds it. What makes 'Fresh Fat' truly distinctive compared with most products made from extrusions is that each piece is unique because of the way it is moulded.

Less likely to come to mind is the type of extrusion that can produce flat sheets, usually of plastic, by feeding material through a slit in a die, then feeding it onto a roller to produce a sheet. As with any extrusion process, the lengths are determined only by where you decide to make a cut.

| Product | Apple iPod Shuffle |
|---|---|
| Designer | Apple design studio |
| Materials | anodised aluminium |
| Date | 2006 |

Apple continually pushes the boundaries of materials and production. This generation of the iPod Shuffle takes a more conventional approach to extrusion (above) than Tom Dixon, maintaining high tolerances while exploiting the ability of extrusion to create a varied profile by using the nib-shaped protrusions as an integral part of the clip.

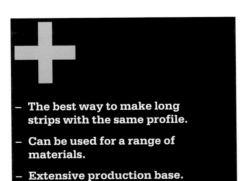

— The best way to make long strips with the same profile.

— Can be used for a range of materials.

— Extensive production base.

— Parts often need to be cut to length, assembled or drilled.

# Pultrusion

Pultrusion is much less common as a plastic-processing method than its more familiar relative, extrusion (see p.78). The processes are similar in that they allow continuous lengths of a set and an unchanging profile to be formed, but one of the main differences between them is that extrusion can be used for aluminiums, wood-based composites and thermoplastics, while pultrusion is used in the forming of composites that use long strands of fibre as reinforcement.

As the name suggests, the process is based on pulling the blended materials of the composite through a heated die. This differs from extrusion, which is based on pushing the material. The continuous lengths of reinforcing fibres, which can be made from glass or carbon, are saturated with a liquid resin mixture as they are pulled through the die, which, besides shaping the component, also acts to cure the resin as it is heated. Sometimes, pre-impregnated ('pre-preg') fibres are used, removing the need for a resin bath.

Manufacturers of plastics have, in recent years, experimented with many applications that traditionally used metals, and pultrusion is a typical example of the benefits such experimentation can bring. Pultruded plastics display an increased range of physical properties that can benefit both engineering and design applications, because they offer the toughness of metals with the advantages of low weight and corrosion-resistance. Pultrusions are incredibly dense, hard and rigid sections – they even 'clank' like pieces of metal when you knock them!

| Product | sample of pultruded plastic |
| --- | --- |
| Materials | glass fibre and polyester resin composite |
| Manufacturer | Fibre Force |
| Country | UK |

These profiles illustrate two of the key properties of pultrusion: first, its ability to produce shapes in plastic having similar properties to metal profiles; secondly, its capacity to have moulded-in colours.

### Volumes of production

Depends on the size and complexity of the shape. 500 metres is a typical minimum run.

### Unit price vs capital investment

The cost is lower than that for some moulding processes, injection (see p.178) and compression moulding (see p.156), for example, but higher than for, say, hand lay-up moulding (see p.134).

### Speed

Depends on size, but, as a rule of thumb, it is possible to achieve 0.5 metres per minute for a profile measuring 50 by 50 millimetres, 0.1 metre per minute for chunky shapes and 1 metre per minute for narrower sections.

### Surface

The surface finish can be controlled to a degree, depending on the reinforcement and polymer.

### Types/complexity of shape

There are no problems with undercuts in pultrusion. Virtually any type of shape that can be squeezed through the die can be made, bearing in mind that the shape must have a constant thickness.

### Scale

The maximum size for profiles is typically 1.2 metres wide, although there are specialist machines that make larger components. Minimum wall thickness is approximately 2.3 millimetres. The size of the manufacturing plant dictates the limit to the length of the pultrusion.

### Tolerances

Vary depending on the profile, but on a standard box-section, with a wall thickness of 4.99 millimetres, the tolerance is ±0.35 millimetres.

### Relevant materials

Any thermoset polymer matrix that can be used with glass and carbon fibre.

### Typical products

Applications for pultrusions are varied and include permanent and temporary structural components for industrial plants, vandal-resistant indoor and outdoor public furniture, and funfair and exhibition stands. Smaller-scale applications include electrically insulated ladders, ski poles, racquet handles, fishing rods and bicycle frames. Perhaps surprisingly, pultruded plastics have a resonance similar to certain woods, which has led to them being used as replacements for hardwood frames for xylophones.

### Similar methods

Extrusion (p.78) and Pulshaping™ (p.84).

### Further information

www.fibreforce.co.uk
www.acmanet.org/pic
www.pultruders.com

1 Individual strands of fibre are fed into a die where they will be soaked in resin and formed into their final profile.

2 A finished tube emerges through the cutter, ready to be cut to length.

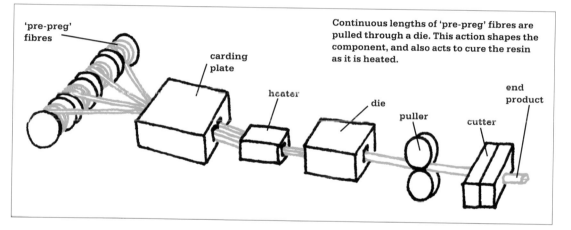

'pre-preg' fibres

carding plate

heater

die

puller

cutter

end product

Continuous lengths of 'pre-preg' fibres are pulled through a die. This action shapes the component, and also acts to cure the resin as it is heated.

- Offers a 75 to 80 per cent weight reduction on steel and 30 per cent on aluminium.

- Greater dimensional stability than its metal counterparts.

- Can be coloured without the problem of chipping because the colour is added to the polymer itself.

- Surface decorations can be applied to mimic grain and other textures.

- Non-conductive and non-corrosive.

- A drawback with pultrusion is that the design is restricted to profiles with a constant cross-section.

# Pulshaping™

Pulshaping™ is one of the newest additions to the manufacturing world and the processing of composites. Developed by US-based Pultrusion Dynamics, Inc., it addresses one of the biggest problems – the constant, unvarying cross-section along the whole length – in the pultrusion process (see p.81). Pulshaping™ allows designers to modify a cross-sectional shape in three dimensions during continuous processing of components in fibre-reinforced plastics. For example, a round profile can be a constant cross-section along the majority of its length, and can then be transformed to a square at one end and an oval at the other, using appropriate tooling. A particular advantage of this process is that it can, for example, allow tube ends to be shaped with threaded fasteners or expansion–reduction couplings joints.

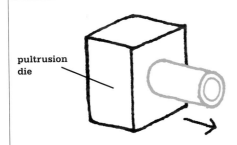

pultrusion die

1  A standard pultrusion die is used to form a cylindrical cross-section.

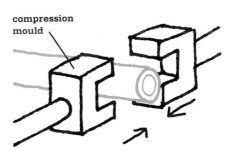

compression mould

2  A two-part compression mould is used to apply pressure and thereby squash the cylindrical walls.

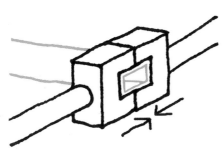

3  The pressure forms the tube into the desired cross-section.

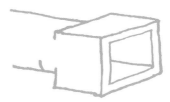

4  The finished part has been 'morphed' from the cylindrical to the new cross-section.

**Volumes of production**

Still in its developmental stage, Pulshaping™, like conventional pultrusion (see p.81), is potentially a high-volume production process.

**Unit price vs capital investment**

Pulshaping™ is a fairly costly process and is not suited to small production runs. Economic quantities are in excess of 2,000 lineal metres.

**Speed**

Typically 0.5–1 metre per minute for the continuous pultrusion part of the process, plus an additional 1–3 minutes for reshaping cycles.

**Surface**

As in pultrusion, the surface finish can be controlled to a slight degree of variation, depending on the reinforcement and polymer. Due to the ability of the process to allow manipulation of form along the cross-section surface, features such as dimples and projections can be designed into the product in the reshaped segment.

**Types/complexity of shape**

This process is highly versatile because of its ability to produce a variety of cross-sectional shapes.

**Scale**

Ideally suited to long products, over 1.8 metres.

**Tolerances**

Very fine tolerances.

**Relevant materials**

Thermosetting resins with glass, carbon or aramid fibre.

**Typical products**

Components such as handles for large tools, which typically require the main body to be straight, with end features to be produced in separate processes, can be made in one go with Pulshaping™.

**Similar methods**

There is nothing really similar to this process in the sense that similar methods, such as extrusion (p.78) and pultrusion (p.81), do not allow for manipulation of the cross-section.

**Further information**

www.pultrusiondynamics.com

---

**+**

- Shares the many advantages listed for pultrusion (see p.81).

- The added advantage is that the geometry can be changed at selected locations along the continuous length of a component.

**–**

- Although the geometry can be altered along the length of the component, this is restricted to a repeat pattern. A continuous curved shape or continuous taper cannot be executed with this method.

# Roll Forming

Roll forming can be used to produce continuous lengths of anything from simple shapes in a single operation to quite complex profiles that require a number of passes through different rollers, from square sections to round shapes and from folded flanges to box sections.

In simple terms, roll forming involves passing a continuous sheet of metal, plastic or even glass, over or through a series of at least two shaped rollers. Feeding the sheet in a straight line between the rollers forces the material to bend into the required profile. The bending occurs progressively over the series of rollers, in a process that may require up to about 25 different rollers, depending on the complexity of the profile. Roll forming can be achieved either as a cold forming process or with heat. In the case of glass, the sheet passes through the rollers as a molten ribbon.

1  A very crude set-up, but this shows a flat strip of metal fed into rollers to be bent into a fairly shallow radius.

2  As the distance between rollers is closed for this second pass through the rollers, so a curve with a tighter radius is achieved.

| Product | Apple iMac aluminium stand |
|---|---|
| Designer | Apple Design Studio |
| Materials | aluminium |
| Date | 2004 |

The aluminium stand for this iMac illustrates, in a discreet way, Apple's achievement in exercising extremely tight control over the manufacturing of their products. The achievement here is in being able to bend such a thick piece of aluminium without any tearing of the material at its widest radius, which would normally be associated with this thickness of material at this scale.

**Volumes of production**
High-volume mass-production.

**Unit price vs capital investment**
Set-up and tooling costs are high, which is why the process is suited to mass-production. It is, however, possible for small prototypes to be produced in a small workshop, depending on the complexity of the shape.

**Speed**
Production speeds are typically 300 to 600 metres per hour for a medium-sized manufacturer, depending on the complexity of the profile and the gauge of the material. Larger manufacturers can often go faster, but minimum quantities and lengths apply.

**Surface**
Other operations, such as punching and embossing, can be incorporated into the process to allow for surface details.

**Types/complexity of shape**
Long lengths of the same profile, which can be quite elaborate.

**Scale**
For mass-produced components the standard depth is approximately 100 millimetres, but it is possible to produce extremely large pieces, as demonstrated by the famous monumental curved steel structures by the artist Richard Serra. In theory, the only thing that dictates the length is the physical size of the manufacturing plant.

**Tolerances**
Vary between ±0.05 and ±1 millimetres, depending on the thickness of the sheet.

**Relevant materials**
Roll forming is almost exclusively used for forming metals, but it is also a useful process for glass and plastics, albeit on a much smaller scale.

**Typical products**
Car parts, architectural profiles, window and picture frames, and guides for sliding doors and curtain rails. In the case of glass, the process is employed to make U-shaped glass profiles that are used in architectural glazing.

**Similar methods**
For metal work, similar methods include sheet-metal forming (p 44) and extrusion (p.78), both of which also provide long lengths of a profiled shape.

**Further information**
www.graphicmetal.com
www.crsauk.com
www.pma.org
www.britishmetalforming.com
www.steelsections.co.uk
www.corusgroup.com

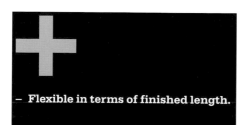

– **Flexible in terms of finished length.**

– **Limited to an unvariable thickness of material.**

# Rotary Swaging
## AKA Radial Forming
## with stationary-spindle and flat swaging

To explain this process in very simple terms, rotary swaging is used to alter the diameter of a range of metal tubing, rods and wires. The process involves the original material being fed through a series of rotating steel dies, which form the material to the required profile (which is always symmetrical and round). As they are rotating, the dies perform a hammering action at a rate of up to approximately 1,000 hits per minute, basically battering the work piece into shape.

Other forms of rotary swaging include stationary-spindle swaging, which is used to form non-round parts. Flat swaging is used to reduce the overall thickness of sheet metal.

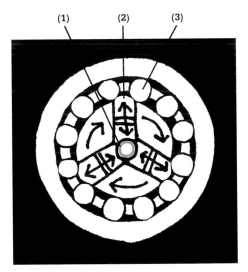

(1)    (2)    (3)

The original-diameter material is fed into a rotating steel die (1). This hammers the material into shape with a series of backers (2), which hit the rollers as the piece rotates. The hammering takes place when the backers pass over a series of rollers (3). Simple centrifugal forces allow the backers to recede from the die before once again being pushed forward as they pass over the rollers.

**Volumes of production**

Medium to high levels of mass-production.

**Unit price vs capital investment**

Although the process sounds complicated, it is actually based around a very simple principle that involves minimal tooling and fast set-up times. This makes it unusual in that it is a high-volume process that is also cost-effective for short runs.

**Speed**

Simple shapes can be produced at a rate of 500 units per hour.

**Surface**

Rotary swaging gives an excellent, shiny surface as a result of the hammering, which acts to buff the surface. The finish is better than stock tubing that has not been swaged.

**Types/complexity of shape**

Because of the action of the rotating tool, options are limited to symmetrical and round shapes. All shapes of tubing, rod and wire can be converted into round profiles using this process, but stationary spindle swaging needs to be used to obtain non-round sections.

**Scale**

Depending on the type of machinery available at the manufacturer, dimensions can vary from 0.5 up to 350 millimetres.

**Tolerances**

Good control of both the inside or outside diameter, depending on how the dies are set up.

**Relevant materials**

Ductile metals are the most commonly used. Ferrous metals with high carbon contents can be problematic.

**Typical products**

Golf clubs, exhaust pipes, screwdriver shanks, furniture legs and rifle barrels.

**Similar methods**

Machining (p.12), impact extrusion (p.128) and deep metal drawing (used to stretch a metal sheet into a variety of hollow shapes, such as cylinders, hemispheres and cups).

**Further information**

www.torrington-machinery.com
www.felss.de
www.elmill.co.uk

- A large range of symmetrical profiles can be formed.

- Because no metal is removed, the process is economical in its use of material.

- It is possible to achieve a fine degree of dimensional control of both the inside and outside surfaces.

- Working the material hardens it, thus increasing its strength.

- Rotary swaging is limited to forming round, symmetrical shapes (stationary-spindle swaging, however, can achieve non-round shapes, including squares and triangles).

- Reduction of diameter tends to be easier at the ends than at the middle of the tubing.

# Pre-Crimp Weaving

Pre-crimp weaving is a great case study in how unexpected materials can be woven and used decoratively. In the same way that soft fabrics are woven for decoration, rigid lengths of wire can be woven to dress and adorn our urban landscapes. Industrial weaving takes many forms, from the chain mail of industrial fencing and fabrics to architectural cladding. Although not recognised as a major industrial process, pre-crimp weaving can be utilised as a way to design large-scale decorative metal screens.

| Product | architectural mesh |
|---|---|
| Materials | stainless steel and brass |
| Manufacturer | Potter & Soar |
| Country | UK |
| Date | 2005 |

Architectural mesh can be produced to a wide range of specifications, to increase or decrease density, texture and transparency. Different optical effects can therefore be created and, in addition, it is self-supporting so it can be used for ceilings and cladding, as well as ornamental balustrading and furniture.

It is a two-step process. The first involves lengths of wire being crimped at specific points. This simple process is based on the wire being fed between two rollers, with teeth biting a kink into the wire at specific distances.

In the second step, the long strands of crimped wire are gathered and fed into an industrial heavy-duty loom, where they are cross-layered with another set of pre-crimped wires and woven into sheets.

1  The lengths of wire are fed into the crimping machine.

2  These toothed cogs show the simple way in which crimping is achieved.

3  Weaving commences on a giant weaving machine.

4  The lengths of woven architectural mesh begin to take shape.

**Volumes of production**

From a minimum of one square metre, which may be expensive, to an unlimited number of sheets.

**Unit price vs capital investment**

Because of the simple wheels used in the crimping, the process does not usually require tooling. The crimping wheels themselves can be cost-effective compared with other types of industrial tooling.

**Speed**

Varies, depending on the type of weave.

**Surface**

Good finish, which can also be electro-polished (a process that removes microscopic amounts of material from the metal).

**Types/complexity of shape**

Flat-sheet post forming can result in infinite possibilities.

**Scale**

The maximum width is 2 metres. The length is restricted by the size of the manufacturer's site.

**Tolerances**

Not applicable.

**Relevant materials**

Typically uses stainless steel 316L, galvanised steel or any weavable alloy.

**Typical products**

Balustrades, external facades, staircase cladding, sunscreens and ceilings that allow for lighting and sprinkler systems to be fitted above.

**Similar methods**

Perforating expanded metal (which uses a single sheet of metal that is then pulled open to create a series of slots, and which is typically seen on the central reservation on motorways) and cable mesh – chain-link fencing that uses wire formed into a spiral, used typically in industrial security fencing.

**Further information**

www.wiremesh.co.uk

– Adaptable, flexible production quantities.

– Produces a self-supporting rigid screen that can be formed and hold its shape.

– Can form only fixed-length panels, as opposed to rolls.

# Veneer Cutting
## including rotary cutting and slicing

| Product | Leonardo lampshade |
|---|---|
| Designer | Antoni Arola |
| Materials | treated wood |
| Manufacturer | Santa & Cole |
| Country | Spain |
| Date | 2003 |

This simple, looped lampshade uses veneers in an unusual, decorative way that draws attention to the surprising translucency of the wood.

It is too obvious to say that trees are one of the richest sources of materials, food and shelter, but, for me, the production of veneers demonstrates the ingenuity and resourcefulness of humans in converting an object into a variety of usable forms. Peeling a tree in continuous strips to create veneers has to be one of the most economical uses for a tree and it unravels the life of the tree in the process, clearly displaying the evidence of its nutrition and lifespan.

There are two main methods for forming veneers: slicing (which involves slicing the tree – or, by now, more likely the log – along its length) and rotary cutting (which involves peeling the log in a continuous strip right into its centre until nothing is left). Rotary cutting is by far the most common form. Harvested logs are sorted according to quality to be used for veneers, pulp or conversion to plywood. Depending on the region in which the logs are gathered, they may need to be scanned for metal content. This can often be the result of bullets lodged in the trees during conflicts.

Once the logs reach the sawmill, they are cut down to the required lengths. These depend on the regional standards and whether a log will be used for veneers, or stuck together to make plywood sheets. The logs are then softened by being soaked in hot water for an average of 24 hours. This loosens the bark and relaxes the fibres in the grain, which makes the peeling process easier.

Once the bark is removed, the logs can be slowly dried before, in rotary cutting, they are set into a machine that rotates them while a cutter is introduced to slowly produce a continuous length of veneer. This length, and those produced by slicing, can be guillotined into shorter lengths.

**Volumes of production**
Not applicable. Since this is a 'commodity', it is just produced all the time.

**Unit price vs capital investment**
Not applicable. Again, veneers are produced all the time, so you only pay for tools and machinery indirectly.

**Speed**
Once loaded into the cutter, a typical birch log (with a 300-millimetre diameter) can be completely 'peeled' in a continuous sheet in less than two minutes.

**Surface**
Considering that the process involves a piece of wood that in essence has been cut with a knife, the surface is fairly smooth. Finer finishing can, obviously, be achieved by sanding.

**Types/complexity of shape**
Thin sheet material.

**Scale**
The blade on the cutter can be set to cut a varying thickness of veneer from approximately 1 to 2 millimetres. The size of the sheet is determined by the width of the log and at which point the veneer is cut into smaller sheets. A typical log 300 millimetres in diameter will produce up to 15 metres of veneer.

**Tolerances**
Not applicable.

**Relevant materials**
Most tree species.

**Typical products**
The obvious use of veneers is in the production of various forms of plywood or veneers for laminating to board for furniture makers. However, there are also companies that laminate veneers with an adhesive and sell them as wall coverings.

**Similar methods**
This is a unique method of processing wood. The veneers, however, can be used to make plywood, which can be formed in a number of ways, including by bending (p.64).

**Further information**
www.ttf.co.uk
www.hpva.org
www.nordictimber.org
www.veneerselector.com

– **Economical use of the material.**

– **Although this is an industrial production method, it has a degree of flexibility, allowing control of the thickness of the veneer and the length and width of the final sheets.**

– **Limited to producing sheets or strips.**

# 4:
# Thin &
# Hollow

## Hollow components with a thin wall section

**The longest chapter in the book, this embraces all sorts of processes for forming hollow and, generally, thin-walled shapes. It discusses the many variations of blow moulding, a process that has been used for several thousand years to produce priceless handblown glassware. The blow-moulding principle has been successfully employed in industrial mass-production, especially by the plastics industry, which spews out millions of disposable bottles for the soft drinks industry. Other forms of casting and moulding are included, from the very common rotational moulding, a form of which is used to produce chocolate Easter eggs, to the less common centrifugal casting that hurls metal or glass around a rotating drum forcing the material to attach itself to the walls, to make anything from small jewellery to huge industrial pipes.**

# Glass Blowing by Hand

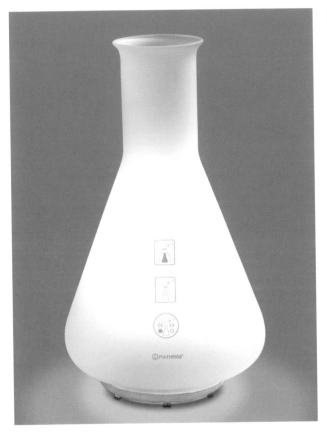

For at least two thousand years, this technique has been used to make anything from tableware to craft pieces. It involves blowing air through a metal tube to inflate a ball of gathered glass at the end of the tube. Before glass blowing, glass objects were produced by dipping a sand core in molten glass prior to rolling it against a flat surface to control the shape. Once cooled, the sand could be removed, leaving a hollow container. With the introduction of the blowing technique came a whole new set of

1   A mass of molten glass is gathered onto the end of a steel tube, ready to be blown.

| Product | **Air Switch flask lamp** |
|---|---|
| Designer | Mathmos Design Studio |
| Materials | acid-etched glass |
| Date | 2004 |

Although this light was handblown, the straight sides and symmetrical shape were achieved by blowing into a mould. Usually, the shape of a handblown piece is controlled only by a series of hand tools as illustrated in the photographs, right.

2   Various hand tools are used to shape the hot glass, in this case a stack of wet fabric.

possibilities, not only in terms of shape but also in terms of widening the availability of this material.

Today, hand-blowing is still used industrially to produce a whole range of products that are blown into moulds, from lighting to wine glasses. Hand-blown glass constitutes a valuable bridge between mass-produced glassware, which requires expensive tooling and very high volumes, and individual one-off pieces.

**Volumes of production**
One-offs and batch production.

**Unit price vs capital investment**
The biggest cost is for the glass-blower's labour. Assuming you want to produce a batch of identical shapes, moulds can be used. Depending on exact quantities, these will be made from materials offering varying degrees of longevity, including wood, plaster or graphite.

**Speed**
Completely dependent on the scale and complexity of the piece, and whether or not the glass is being blown into a mould.

**Surface**
Excellent.

**Types/complexity of shape**
For free-blown glass, virtually any shape is possible.

**Scale**
As big as the lungs of the glass-blower will allow, bearing in mind that the blower also needs to wrestle with the weight of the glass at the end of the tube.

**Tolerances**
Difficult to be precise, because it is a handmade process.

**Relevant materials**
Any type of glass.

**Typical products**
Anything from tableware to sculptures.

**Similar methods**
Lampworking (p.100) and machine-blown glass made using blow and blow (p.102) or press and blow (p.106) moulding.

**Further information**
www.nazeing-glass.com
www.kostaboda.se
www.glassblowers.org/
www2.cemr.wvu.edu/~wwwpwi/glass
www.handmade-glass.com

- Flexible enough to produce different shapes.
- Can be used for one-off, batch or medium-volume production.

- Units can be expensive due to labour costs.

# Lampworking Glass Tube

There are hundreds of ways of hand-working glass, employing both hot and cold (cutting, for example) processes for making objects without the need for tooling. Lampworking involves the localised heating of a piece of glass to allow it to be pushed, pulled and generally shaped by a skilled craftsman. The process can be seen as providing a third alternative for shaping glass somewhere between expensive hand forming and mass-production that requires tooling. It is a process that is ideally suited to short production runs.

The process starts with a hollow tube of glass, which is set into a slowly rotating lathe. Heat from a blowlamp is applied to specific areas, which are then pushed with a wooden former. Lampworking involves soft, malleable glass being pushed into shape. Depending on whether closed or open forms are required, ends can be left open or rolled round and sealed off.

| Product | thin-walled vases |
|---|---|
| Designer | Olgoj Chorchoj |
| Materials | borosilicate glass |
| Country | Czech Republic |
| Date | 2001 |

These elegant vases illustrate the complexity of components that can be formed using this method. The internal opaque white form and the transparent external tube were made separately and joined together later on a lathe.

A tube of glass being locally heated while rotating on the lathe, before the wooden former is introduced.

## Volumes of production

One of the best things about this type of semi-manual process is that there is no limit to the numbers of units that can be produced – it can be used for anything from one-offs to runs of several thousand. If you want to produce more than 1,000 units, then it might be worth considering having the product blown using a semi-automated set-up.

## Unit price vs capital investment

Unit price is relatively low for a product that can be tailored and easily adapted. Capital investment is non-existent because there are no tools.

## Speed

Varies, depending on the complexity of the shape.

## Surface

Excellent.

## Types/complexity of shape

Limits to the shape are based on symmetry because of the fact that the glass tube rotates around a single axis. However, post working of the glass once it is taken off the lathe can allow for design details to be added. Laboratory glassware is made using this method, which may give you an idea of its complexity. Wall sections are generally thin.

## Scale

The scale of products is limited by the type of lathe and the skill of the craftsman.

## Tolerances

Because this is a hand-worked process, tolerances are not very high.

## Relevant materials

Mainly restricted to borosilicate glass.

## Typical products

Anything from special laboratory apparatus and packaging, to oil and vinegar containers (the kind you find in expensive delis, where the vinegar bottle is trapped inside the oil bottle), thermometers and lighting.

## Similar methods

Glass blowing by hand (p.98)

## Further information

www.asgs-glass.org
www.bssg.co.uk

---

- Highly versatile process.

- Shapes can be varied even within the same batch.

- Cost-effective for experiments and prototypes.

- Complex shapes can be formed.

- This type of process for making glassware is generally used to make batch-produced products without requiring any investment in tooling.

---

- Not cost-effective for large production runs.

# Glass Blow and Blow Moulding

There are a number of different ways in which blowing air into, or out of, a material can be used to manufacture products, many of which are described in this book. Although varieties of blow moulding can be used for plastic (see, for example, injection blow moulding, p.111) and even – on a limited scale – metal (see inflating metal, p.62, and superforming aluminium, p.56), it remains one of the major industrial mass-production methods for making blown glass objects. The industrial blow moulding of glass today consists of two main methods: blow and blow, and press and blow (see p.106). The blow and blow method discussed here is used to make bottles with narrow necks, such as wine bottles. The term 'blown glass' can, of course, also be applied to one-off handmade pieces (see glass blowing by hand, p.98), but we are talking here about the sort of large-scale process that is capable of producing hundreds of thousands of units per day.

| Product | Kikkoman bottle |
|---|---|
| Designer | Kenji Ekuan |
| Materials | soda-lime glass |
| Manufacturer | Kikkoman Corporation |
| Country | Japan |
| Date | 1961 |

The proportions and narrow neck of this classic soy sauce bottle are typical of the blow and blow process for glass forming. The parting lines, which are just visible, show the point where the two halves of the mould have separated. The red plastic cap is injection moulded.

To form a product using blow and blow moulding, a mixture of sand, sodium carbonate and calcium carbonate is carried to the top level of the factory, where it is heated to 1,550°C in a furnace that can be as large as a small living room. The molten glass is released in a series of fat sausage shapes, known as 'gobs', which are drawn down by gravity into the forming machines. At this stage, air is injected into the gob to partially form the bottle, including the neck. This semi-formed glass is then removed, rotated 180 degrees and clamped into a further mould. At this stage, air is injected into the mould to form the final shape. The various parts of the mould then open and the bottle is lifted onto a conveyor belt, which carries it to an annealing oven to eliminate any tension in the glass.

### Volumes of production

Range from several thousand to hundreds of thousands per 24-hour period. The minimum production run to achieve an economical price is approximately 50,000 units. The weight of the glass, however, is one of the main determinants of speed, and rates of 170,000 units per day are not uncommon.

### Unit price vs capital investment

This is a process for high-volume mass-production. Tooling costs are high, and production runs for glass need to last for days, on a continuous 24-hour cycle, for the products to be cost-effective.

### Speed

Depending on the bottle size, machines can be set up to hold several moulds at the same time on a single machine. This can result in very high production rates, with some approaching 15,000 pieces an hour.

### Surface

Excellent finish – look at any wine bottle.

### Types/complexity of shape

Restricted to fairly simple forms. In large-scale glass production, the forms need to be carefully designed to allow for the easy opening of moulds – for instance, they cannot have sharp corners, undercuts or large, flat areas. The blow and blow method is, in fact, very inflexible, and you should consult a manufacturer for specific designs.

Do not look at expensive perfume bottles for inspiration, because that is a different game altogether.

### Scale

Because of the nature of the applications for blow-moulded products (mainly for domestic glass vessels), most manufacturing is set up for a maximum of 300 millimetre high containers.

### Relevant materials

Almost any type of glass.

### Typical products

Narrow-necked wine and spirit bottles, and oil, vinegar and champagne bottles.

### Similar methods

While this method is suited to making narrow-necked glass containers, press and blow moulding can make open-necked glass containers (p.106). For plastics, see injection blow moulding (p.111) and extrusion blow moulding (p.114).

### Further information

www.vetreriebruni.com
www.saint-gobain-emballage.fr
www.packaging-gateway.com
www.glassassociation.org.uk
www.glasspac.com
www.beatsonclark.co.uk

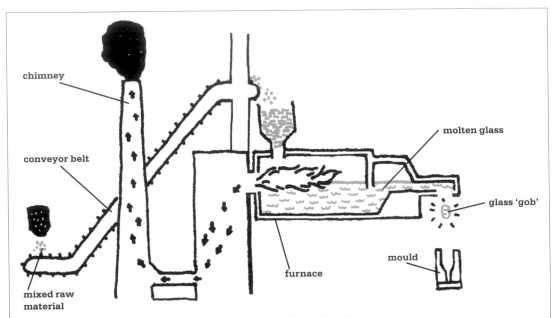

chimney

conveyor belt

molten glass

glass 'gob'

mould

furnace

mixed raw
material

1  A mixture of sand, sodium carbonate and calcium carbonate is fed, via
a conveyor belt, into a furnace at the top of the factory. Here, it is heated
to make molten glass. This molten glass is released through a series of
slides, and, through gravity, falls into a fat sausage shape, called a gob.

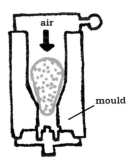

air

mould

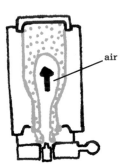

air

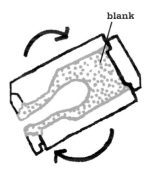

blank

2  Blown down into the mould,
the gob is the starting point for
the bottle.

3  Air is injected into the neck to
make a partially formed blank,
including the neck.

4  The blank is rotated 180° and
transferred to a second mould.

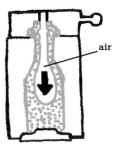

air

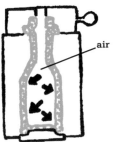

air

5  More air is injected.

6  Air is injected until the glass is
blown to form the final shape,
with the glass walls at the
correct thickness.

7  The glass bottle is lifted out
of the mould.

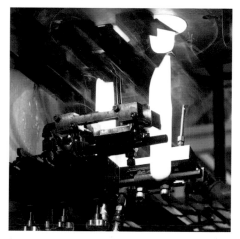

1  Gobs of heated glass are dropped from an elevated furnace.

2  The glass gobs are cut to length before being dropped into the mould.

3  Hot bottles leaving the mould.

4  A series of eight moulding machines feed bottles onto the production line, ready for annealing.

– Very low unit price.

– Able to make narrow-necked containers.

– Exceptionally fast rates of production.

– Versatility is very low in this high-volume method of production.

– Very high tooling costs.

– Demands very high volumes.

– Limited to fairly simple hollow forms.

– Adding colour to glass can be expensive as it involves 'running through' colours at the end of production to ensure that there is no bleeding between colours.

# Glass Press and Blow Moulding

A form of industrial glass blow moulding, the technique known as 'press and blow' is used to make wide-mouthed containers such as jam jars, rather than the narrow-necked items, such as wine bottles, that are made with the blow and blow process (see p.102). The main difference between the techniques occurs during the moulding process. Instead of being blown, to create wide-mouthed vessels the 'gob' of glass is pressed onto a male former inside the mould cavity. This can speed up production cycles and allows greater control in the distribution of the glass, so that a thinner wall can be achieved. After the objects have been formed, the production line pushes them into an annealing furnace where, over the period of an hour, the objects are slowly cooled to room temperature, thus eliminating any tension in the glass.

Inside the factories, machines shoot out glowing, molten gobs of glass that look like shafts of light falling into the cavities of the empty moulds. This process has none of the theatre and craftsmanship of hand-blown glass: the automated, greasy, noisy, steaming machines can turn out hundreds of thousands of bottles per day with just a handful of men watching over this vast production.

Compared with the blow and blow process, which can produce over 350,000 narrow-necked units per day, this process can churn out 400,000

| Product | storage jar |
|---|---|
| Materials | soda lime glass with thermoplastic elastomer (TPE) seal |
| Manufacturer | Vetrerie Bruni |
| Country | Italy |

The open necked shape of this jar is a typical example of a product for which you would have to consider press and blow moulding in preference to blow and blow moulding (see p.102).

units the size of, for example, jam jars. When it comes to small 'press and blow' bottles, however, the machines can pump out up to 900,000 units of, say, small pharmaceutical bottles per day, running on a continuous 24-hour cycle. Uninterrupted production runs for some food packaging can last up to ten months, just producing the same objects over and over again.

## Volumes of production

Range from several thousand to hundreds of thousands per day. This level of high-volume production is usually determined by time, rather than by numbers of units produced per hour. It may take up to eight hours for production to be in full swing, so a minimum production cycle is likely to be around three days, with machines running without interruption.

## Unit price vs capital investment

As with the similar process of blow and blow moulding (see p.102), this is a process only for high volume mass-production. Tooling is prohibitively expensive unless you have production runs running in to several tens of thousands of units.

## Speed

The press and blow method is generally slightly faster than blow and blow glass production, though they have in common the fact that the weight of the glass is a determining factor for speed. Rates of 250,000 units per day for a typical large cooking-sauce jar are fairly standard.

## Surface

Just look at a jam jar and you can see the excellent finish. However, just as with blow and blow bottles, the witness lines will need to be taken into account if labels are to be added.

## Types/complexity of shape

Restricted to fairly simple forms with wide, open necks. In large-scale glass production these forms cannot have sharp corners, undercuts or large, flat areas, all of which would make releasing them from the mould difficult. Compared with blow and blow moulding, press and blow allows a greater degree of control over the thickness of the glass.

## Scale

As with blow and blow, manufacturing is set up for a maximum of 300-millimetre-high containers.

## Relevant materials

Almost any type of glass.

## Typical products

Open-necked jam jars and spirit bottles, open-necked pharmaceutical and other containers, and food packaging,

## Similar methods

For glass, blow and blow moulding (p.102), lampworking (p.100) and glass blowing by hand (p.98). For plastics, plastic blow moulding (p.109) and extrusion blow moulding (p.114).

## Further information

www.vetreriebruni.com
www.britglass.org.uk
www.saint-gobain-conditionnement.com
www.beatsonclark.co.uk

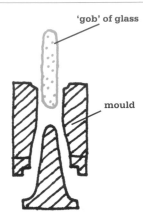

'gob' of glass

mould

1  Machines shoot out molten 'gobs' of glass, each falling above an empty mould.

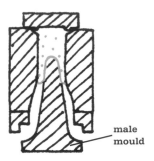
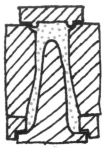

male mould

2  The male part of the mould begins to shape the glass as it falls.

3  The soft glass is pressed right down into the mould to form a blank.

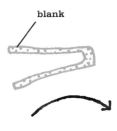

blank

4  The blank is rotated 180 degrees.

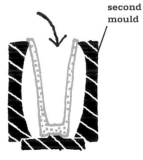

second mould

5  The blank is transferred into a second mould.

air

6  Air is used to blow the glass right into the mould to form the final shape.

- **Very low unit price.**

- **Suited to making thin-walled, open-necked vessels.**

- **Exceptionally fast rates of production.**

- **Exceptionally fast cycle times.**

- **Very high tooling costs.**

- **Limited to fairly simple hollow forms.**

- **Adding colour to glass can be expensive, as can running through colours at the end of production to clean out the machines.**

- **Demands high volumes in order to be economical.**

# Plastic Blow Moulding

Blow moulding is an umbrella term that describes one of the major industrial mass-production methods for producing a whole host of hollow products. In one sense it is unusual, because it is a process that can be used for moulding plastic containers as well as glass bottles (see glass blow and blow [p.102] and glass press and blow [p.106] moulding).

There are several forms of blow moulding suitable for plastics, including injection blow moulding and injection stretch moulding (see p.111), and extrusion and co-extrusion blow moulding (see p.114). All have differing potential to create shapes, but, in simple terms, all of them involve a process that is like blowing a balloon into a mould to form a shape. The process starts with a pre-form being fed into a two-part mould. The closing of the mould snips the material to an appropriate length, forming a seal at one end of the plastic. This pipe-like form is fed into a second mould where air is blown into it, forcing the plastic to expand against the mould cavity to form the final shape, after which the mould opens and the part is released.

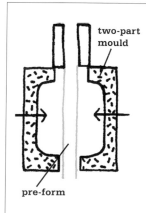
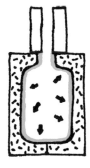

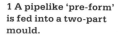

1 A pipelike 'pre-form' is fed into a two-part mould.

2 The mould closes, snipping the material to an appropriate length and forming a seal at one end of the plastic.

3 Air is blown into the pre-form, forcing the plastic to expand against the mould cavity to form the final shape.

4 The mould opens and the part is released.

### Volumes of production

Depending on the size and the material, blow moulding can be an extremely rapid form of production, with an output of from approximately 500 units per hour to over a million units per 24-hour cycle. To get the most out of the process, in terms of cost savings, production should run into the hundreds of thousands.

### Unit price vs capital investment

Unit prices for most standard blow-moulded parts are very low, which is best comprehended by looking at the volume of cheap products and packaging that is produced with this process. This economy of scale is counterbalanced, of course, by the extremely high tooling costs.

### Speed

Small containers can be produced on multi-cavity moulds to yield approximately 60,000 small (less than, say, 700 millilitres) polyethylene terephthalate (PET) bottles per hour.

### Surface

Excellent finish, but parting lines remain down the length.

### Types/complexity of shape

Depending on the specific process, blow-moulded shapes are generally simple and rounded. Although products can be produced with no draft angles, manufacturers prefers a small draft.

### Scale

From small cosmetics bottles to parts that weigh over 25 kilograms.

### Relevant materials

The typically waxy, high-density polyethylene (HDPE) is one of the most common materials used for this process. Other materials include polypropylene, polyethylene, polyethylene terephthalate (PET) and polyvinyl chloride (PVC).

### Typical products

The chances are that in the average household you will have at least one large cupboard full of different plastic containers that are blow moulded. Basically, blow-moulded items include everything from plastic milk cartons and shampoo bottles to toys, toothpaste tubes, detergent bottles, watering cans and – outside the home – car fuel tanks.

### Similar methods

Stretch moulding, extrusion blow moulding (p.114), injection blow moulding and co-extrusion blow moulding (p.114).

### Further information

www.rpc-group.com
www.bpf.co.uk

- **Very low unit price.**
- **Exceptionally fast rates of production.**
- **Details, such as threads, can be moulded in.**

- **High tooling costs.**
- **Demands high volumes in order to be cost-effective.**
- **Limited to fairly simple hollow forms.**

# Injection Blow Moulding
## with injection stretch moulding

Injection blow moulding is most easily described as being a subdivision of plastic blow moulding (see p.109), the process that works on the same principle as blowing up a balloon, but into a mould that forms the shape.

As the name implies, this is a two-step moulding process that offers a number of advantages over other forms of blow moulding because it is possible to create far more complex shapes around the neck of the moulded part. A hollow pre-form is made using injection moulding (see p.178), which allows for the moulding of a complex thread at the neck. The pre-form is placed into the mould cavity where it is blown with air, forcing the plastic against the mould cavity.

Using an injection-moulded pre-form, means that this method offers a greater degree of stability and control over the shape than extrusion blow moulding (see p.114), although the choice of suitable materials is more limited.

Injection stretch moulding is a method used for high-end products (such as bottles) made from polyethylene terephthalate (PET) which uses a rod to stretch a pre-form into the mould before blowing.

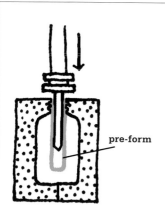
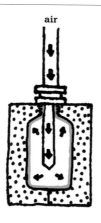

1  An injection-moulded pre-form is placed in the mould.

2  Compressed air is injected, blowing the pre-form into the mould cavity to form the final shape.

3  The mould opens and the part is released.

| Product | **injection-moulded pre-form (left) and blow-moulded bottle (right)** |
| --- | --- |
| Materials | polyethylene terephthalate (PET) |
| Country | Germany |

This pre-form and the resulting blown bottle show, in very simple terms, how straightforward the process is that forms the billions of plastic bottles that litter our urban landscape. The advantage of using injection moulding is demonstrated by the detailed thread that has been formed around the neck of the pre-form.

### Volumes of production

Injection blow moulding is ideally suited to high-volume production, which often runs into millions of units.

### Unit price vs capital investment

Costly tooling, for both the injecting and blowing parts of the process, as well as substantial set-up charges. However, unit prices can be extremely low because of the volumes produced, and this justifies the high initial costs.

### Speed

The various forms of blow moulding are difficult to pin down in terms of speed of production due to variables such as part size and the number of mould cavities in operation. A typical 150 millilitre bottle, however, can be produced by injection blow moulding in an eight-cavity mould at the rate of 2,400 units per hour.

### Surface

Excellent finish.

### Types/complexity of shape

Injection blow moulding is suited to fairly simple shapes, which have a large radius and consistent wall thicknesses over the whole product.

### Scale

Typically used for containers of less than 250 millilitres.

### Relevant materials

Compared with extrusion blow moulding (see p.114), this method is suited to more rigid materials such as polycarbonate (PC) and polyethylene terephthalate (PET). It is, however, often used for non-rigid materials, such as polyethylene (PE).

### Typical products

Small shampoo, detergent and other bottles.

### Similar methods

Extrusion blow moulding (p.114) for plastic, and press and blow moulding (p.106) for glass.

### Further information

www.rpc-group.com
www.bpf.co.uk

- Very low unit price.
- Exceptionally fast rates of production.
- Suited to small containers.
- Allows greater control over neck design, weight and wall thickness than other blow-moulding methods.

- Higher tooling costs than in extrusion blow moulding (see p.114).
- Demands high volumes.
- Limited to fairly simple hollow forms.

# Extrusion Blow Moulding
## with co-extrusion blow moulding

Extrusion blow moulding is part of the plastic blow moulding group of processes (see p.109). In this particular method, the plastic is extruded (see extrusion, p.78) into a sausage shape known as a 'lug' and pinched into short lengths as it drops into the mould cavity. Here, it is blown with air, forcing the plastic against the mould cavity to form the final shape. The process leaves excess 'pinched' material (a 'tail'), which must be removed – though evidence of it can be seen in the finished product, on the underside of any shampoo bottle, for example.

In co-extrusion blow moulding different materials are combined to form a multi-layered product.

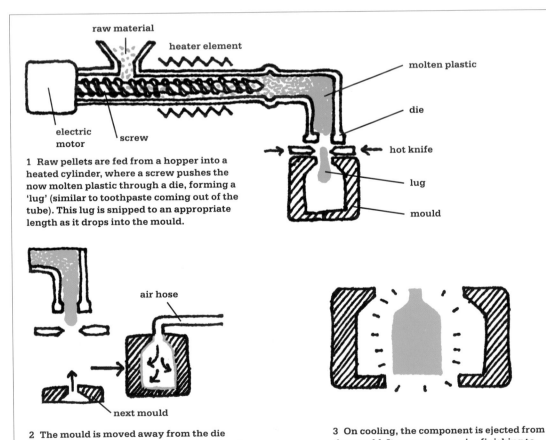

1  Raw pellets are fed from a hopper into a heated cylinder, where a screw pushes the now molten plastic through a die, forming a 'lug' (similar to toothpaste coming out of the tube). This lug is snipped to an appropriate length as it drops into the mould.

2  The mould is moved away from the die and air is injected, inflating the material and pushing it against the walls of the mould.

3  On cooling, the component is ejected from the mould. It may now require finishing to remove the 'tail'.

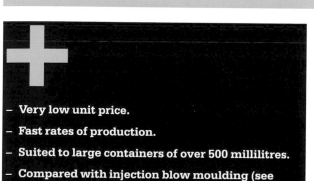

**Volumes of production**

Unlike injection blow moulding (see p.111), which offers the possibility of production runs extending into the millions, extrusion blow moulding can be used on much shorter runs, sometimes as low as 20,000.

**Unit price vs capital investment**

Although lower in cost than injection blow moulding (by about a third), it is still an expensive set-up.

**Speed**

As with other, similar methods, the production rate is determined by the weight of the part: a typical 5-litre container can be produced at a rate of 1,000 per hour (using a single machine, with four moulds running concurrently). Blow-moulded milk bottles of the sort found in supermarkets can be made at a rate of around 2,000 units per hour.

**Surface**

Excellent finish.

**Types/complexity of shape**

Extrusion blow moulding is suited to the production of larger and more complex shapes than injection blow moulding, notably the integrated handles on plastic milk containers, or on the large petrol containers you can find in filling-stations.

**Scale**

Although it is capable of producing products such as shampoo bottles, extrusion blow moulding is also suitable for small runs and can be used to make products at the larger end of the blow-moulding scale, typically over 500 millilitres.

**Relevant materials**

Polypropelene (PP), polyethylene (PE), polyethylene terephthalate (PET) and polyvinyl chloride (PVC).

**Typical products**

Extrusion blow moulding is best suited to larger products, which might typically include toys, oil drums and car fuel tanks, and large detergent bottles.

**Similar methods**

Injection blow moulding (p.111) and rotational moulding (p.119).

**Further information**

www.rpc-group.com
www.bpf.co.uk
www.weltonhurst.co.uk

- Very low unit price.

- Fast rates of production.

- Suited to large containers of over 500 millilitres.

- Compared with injection blow moulding (see p.111), extrusion blow moulding is capable of producing more complex shapes.

- Lower tooling costs than for injection blow moulding.

- Demands high volumes.

# Dip Moulding

Dipping a shape into a material that has been melted (or is in an otherwise liquid state) is possibly one of the oldest methods of forming shapes. It is also one of the simplest techniques to understand, and, in terms of tools and moulds, it is one of the cheapest methods of producing plastic products.

To be presented with a ceramic former, such as the one illustrated here, is to be given a gem from the usually hidden world of manufacturing. Artists (particularly Rachel Whiteread in her award-winning 1993 concrete sculpture *House*) have often explored the negative spaces within our environments. In a similar way, these little gems give us a unique view into the world of production from an angle

| Product | balloon former (far left) and balloon (left) |
|---|---|
| Designer | Michael Faraday created the first rubber balloon in 1824 |
| Materials | earthenware ceramic former; latex balloon |
| Manufacturer | Wade Ceramics Limited (balloon former) |

The simple ceramic former perfectly illustrates the principle behind dip moulding, showing how hollow products – such as this party balloon – are made.

that is rarely seen. The bulbous shape triggers a small flash of recognition, but you cannot quite put your finger on what it is until someone tells you that the shapes are ceramic formers for making balloons.

In principle, the process of dip moulding is incredibly straightforward. As the name suggests, you simply dip a former into a liquid polymer bath, let it cure and peel it off. In reality, it is a little bit more complex than that, because dip moulding is a process that can be adapted to many different materials and set-ups, although the basic idea stays the same.

### Volumes of production
From batch production to high-volume mass-production.

### Unit price vs capital investment
One of the least expensive ways of mass-producing plastic components, with reasonably cheap tooling and easy-to-produce samples, while still allowing for cost-effective unit parts.

### Speed
This process involves many steps, including pre-heating of the former, dipping, curing and finally peeling the finished moulding from the former, which makes for a slow process if performed manually. Complex mouldings may take up to 45 minutes to complete, while the production of very simple shapes, such as end caps (for example, simple bicycle-handlebar grips) can be fully automated and may take only 30 seconds.

### Surface
The exterior of the component is determined by the natural state of the material, and may have a small nipple as evidence of the dripping polymer from the mould.

### Types/complexity of shape
Soft, rubbery, flexible, though simple, forms. Products must be shaped in such a way that they can be unpeeled from the mould.

### Scale
The scale of dip mouldings is theoretically only limited by the size of the bath containing the polymer, but generally mouldings range from 1-millimetre diameter end caps to 600-millimetre industrial pipe covers.

### Tolerances
Dip moulding does not achieve a high level of accuracy, apart from on the internal dimensions.

### Relevant materials
Because of the nature of the process, which involves the former being 'undressed' as the part is removed, it is limited to soft materials and parts that can be stretched over the moulds, including PVC, latex, polyurethanes, elastomers and silicones.

### Typical products
A whole range of flexible and semi-rigid products, from kitchen and surgical gloves to balloons and those soft, waxy plastic handlebar grips for children's bikes.

### Similar methods
An economical alternative to plastic blow moulding (p.109) and rotational moulding (p.119).

### Further information
www.wjc.co.uk
www.uptechnology.com
www.wade.co.uk
www.qualatex.com

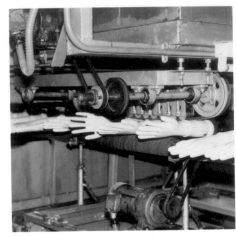

1  An automated production line showing the dipping of ceramic formers to make rubber gloves.

2  The rubber gloves being dried.

3  A vat of sky-blue latex being used to produce party balloons.

– Highly cost-effective for short production runs.

– A prototype former and sample mouldings can be produced in a matter of days.

– Limited to simple shapes.

# Rotational Moulding
## AKA Roto Moulding and Rotational Casting

Rotational moulding is all about making things that are hollow. If you have ever wanted to know how chocolate Easter eggs are made, then the answer lies in this method of production. One of the interesting things about rotational moulding is that the soft and rounded products that are typical of this method very much take their aesthetic from the limitations of the process. This is quite unlike injection moulding (see p.178), which uses pressure to inject material into the mould, producing sharp edges and fine detail. Roto moulding, as it is sometimes known, uses only heat and the rotation of a mould to form parts and thus lacks the fineness of pressure-formed parts.

In a sense, rotational moulding is based on a similar idea to ceramic slip casting (see p.122). In both methods, a liquid material is built up on the internal cavity of a mould, allowing the manufacture of hollow parts. It is a simple, four-stage process, which begins with adding powdered polymer to a cold die. The amount of powder in relation to the size of the die determines the wall thickness of the final component. The second stage involves the die being uniformly heated inside an oven, while simultaneously being slowly rotated around two axes. This allows the polymer (which is now liquid) to tumble around the inside of the die, where it builds up on the walls and creates a hollow form. Finally, while the die is still rotating, it is

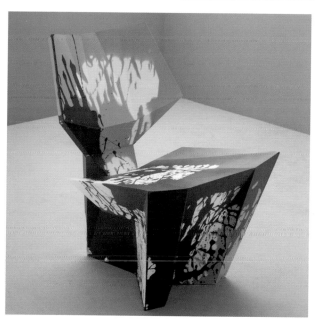

| Product | Pollock chair |
| --- | --- |
| Designers | Tom Vaughan and William Smith |
| Materials | polyethylene |
| Manufacturer | designers' own production |
| Country | UK |
| Date | 2004 |

The sharp angles seen on the edges of this chair are an uncommon feature of a process that normally produces parts with big, soft radiuses. They are, however, testament to the low cost, angular, folded aluminium sheet that was used to make the mould. An additive was used to help the flow of plastic into the tight corners and avoid the air bubbles that are normally a feature of sharp edges. The splattered 'Pollock' decoration was achieved by the material being thrown against the mould wall as it was spinning at a faster than normal rate.

cooled using air or water before the component is removed.

The Pollock chair illustrated here tells an unusual story of a 'back-garden shed industry' which uses gaffer tape and a variety of sheet materials to turn the conventional and widespread rotational moulding process on its head. The initial shape of the chair was constructed in sketch form using folded card. Once the final shape was decided upon the chair was made again using more resilient polypropylene sheet, which was copied to form an aluminium net – a flat cut-out of a three-dimensional shape which is

### Volumes of production
From batch production to high-volume mass-production.

### Unit price vs capital investment
Less expensive to set up and operate than injection moulding (see p.178). Because there is no pressure involved, moulds are simpler and cheaper. Unit costs are still very low.

### Speed
This is affected by the size of the component and the wall thickness, both of which affect the cooling-cycle time. Some components, such as plastic drums for storing liquids, may require entry and exit holes for the liquid to be cut by hand.

### Surface
The internal surface may reveal the swirls of the plastic as it was being formed, similar to the swirls of chocolate you can see on the inside of an Easter egg. The surface that is in contact with the mould is of much higher quality. While it may not be possible to achieve a super-glossy finish, matt finishes can be built into the mould to hide small defects. Inserts with graphics on can also be moulded into parts.

### Types/complexity of shape
Adaptable to a range of shapes. Even undercuts are possible. Wall thickness should be kept uniform, between approximately 2 and 15 millimetres. Unlike with other processes, there can be a build-up of material in corners which makes them the strongest part of the component.

### Scale
Starting with chocolate eggs, it is possible to manufacture hollow products up to 7 metres long by 4 metres wide, such as panels for workmen's temporary huts.

### Tolerances
Compared with other plastic moulding methods, tolerances are low due to shrinkage, cooling rates and the wall thickness, which varies slightly across the moulding.

### Relevant materials
Polyethylene, which has that Edam-cheesy feel, is a common material for rotational moulding. Other resins can also be used, including acrylonitrile butadiene styrene (ABS), polycarbonate, nylon, polypropylene and polystyrene. Reinforcement fibres can also be introduced to increase strength in the final component.

### Typical products
Chocolate eggs, plastic road-traffic cones, portable toilets, tool cases, large toys that take up half your living room, as well as many other hollow products.

### Similar methods
Centrifugal casting (p.143) is a similar process for plastics, but it is not widely available and can only produce small parts. Also blow moulding in all its forms (pp.102–115, and dip moulding (p.116).

### Further information
www.bpf.co.uk/bpfgroups/rotamoulding
   _group.cfm
www.rotomolding.org

folded together. It is the use of this aluminium net, which was folded into a three-dimensional hollow form to create a mould, that marks the real innovation in the project allowing a product with sharp corners to be made.

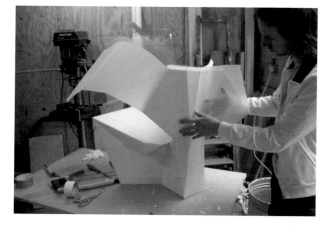

- Ideal for hollow shapes.
- Suitable for low-volume production.
- Simple process.
- Allows for cost-effective production of large components.

- Not suitable for making small, precise components.

These three images, showing the manual, experimental, almost home-made nature of this particular project, the Pollock chair, perfectly capture the essence of rotational moulding.

# Slip Casting

This is a manufacturing process that is just as likely to be used in a college foundation art and design course as in the industrial workshops of Wedgwood or Royal Doulton. In slip casting, ceramic particles are first suspended in water to form 'slip', which is something like the colour and consistency of melted chocolate. This slip is tipped into a plaster mould. Because the dry plaster mould is porous, the liquid is absorbed from the outer layers of the slip, leaving a coating of leathery and hard ceramic

| Product | Wedgwood teapot, before finishing |
|---|---|
| Materials | bone china |
| Manufacturer | Wedgwood |
| Country | UK |

It is often the unfinished article that best reveals the production process, rather than the finished product. This image was taken while the clay was still wet, before the excess material at the top is trimmed off. The parting lines, where the two halves of the mould met, are still visible on the sides of the teapot.

on the inner surface of the mould. When a sufficient thickness has built up, the mould is turned upside down and the remaining muddy liquid is poured out. The excess ceramic around the opening of the mould is trimmed to produce a clean edge before the mould is opened and the moulding, now in its 'green' state, is removed, ready for firing.

Pressure-assisted slip casting (see p.208) is a process that is employed for larger components.

### Volumes of production

Versatile production volumes – anything from small-scale craft batch production to factory production.

### Unit price vs capital investment

Slip casting is economical for small quantities because inexpensive moulds can be made in small workshops while maintaining fairly low unit prices. However, in industrial production the plaster moulds have a limited life and need to be replaced after approximately 100 castings.

### Speed

Slip casting can be summarised by saying that 'time equals thickness'. Because of the number of operations and drying times involved, even as an industrial process slip casting still has one foot in the craft tradition, with a fair degree of labour involved.

### Surface

Slip casting is a great process for achieving surface patterns on objects (such as raised flower patterns). As with all ceramic products, glazing is required.

### Types/complexity of shape

Shapes can range from small and simple to large and complex, and can include parts with undercuts. Anything from bathroom products to art objects and dinnerware can be made with this process.

### Scale

Large moulds can become very heavy and, given the massive amount of slip that would be needed to fill the void, slip casting may not be suited to large shapes. There is also a need for a kiln that is large enough to fire the finished product. Products such as tableware represent the average size.

### Tolerances

It is hard to achieve high tolerances because the parts shrink considerably during firing and, even before that, inside the mould as the water is being drawn out of the slip.

### Relevant materials

All types of ceramic.

### Typical products

Slip casting is used to make any type of hollow product, from one-off pieces of tableware such as teapots, vases and figurines to high volumes of sanitary ware.

### Similar methods

Pressure-assisted slip casting (p.208) and tape casting (a process used for making multilayered capacitors for the electronics industry, involving laying down thin sheets of ceramic-loaded polymers that are laminated with other materials).

### Further information

www.ceramfed.co.uk
www.cerameunie.net

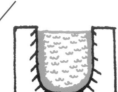

slip    plaster mould

1 Slip is poured into a plaster mould, which absorbs the water leaving a layer of hard, leathery ceramic.

2 The slip is allowed to sit in the mould until a sufficient thickness has built up.

3 The mould is turned upside down and any remaining muddy liquid is poured out.

4 The excess ceramic around the opening of the mould is trimmed to produce a clean edge before the product is released for firing.

1 Empty plaster moulds.

2 Moulds filled with slip.

**+**

- Ideal for producing hollow ware.
- Complex forms can easily be achieved.
- Efficient use of material.
- Lends itself well to low-production runs.

**−**

- Labour-intensive.
- Limited control over tolerances.
- Slow production rate.
- Large-scale production requires many moulds, which themselves require storage.

# Hydroforming Metal
## AKA Fluid Forming

Hydroforming is a fairly new process for forming steel and other metals. It works by forcing a water and oil solution into a cylinder, or other closed shape, that is confined by a die. In essence, the process makes it possible to 'inflate' metal tubes and form metal sheets into elaborate shapes by forcing them against a die. The water pressure of up to 15,000 psi expands the material, forcing it to conform to the shape of the die to form the required component.

Tubes and cylinders are the most common starting points for hydroforming, although panel hydroforming at high pressures also exists for forming pillow shapes from two panels sealed together.

A number of benefits have resulted from this process, including parts with reduced weight and faster production times than with similar methods, such as superforming aluminium (see p.56) and inflating metal (see p.62). In order for the full potential of hydroforming to be exploited, designers need to think of it as a way of reducing costs by making something from a single material rather than having to produce a multitude of parts that need to be joined together.

| Product | t-section of a concept for a handrail system |
|---|---|
| Designers | Amelie Bunte, Anette Ströh, André Saloga and Robert Franzheld, students at the Bauhaus University in Weimar; engineering by Kristof Zientz and Karsten Naunheim, students at Darmstadt University of Technology |
| Materials | hydroformed powder-coated steel; stainless steel tubes |
| Manufacturer | college project |
| Country | Germany |
| Date | 2005 |

This deceptively simple, white-powder-coated steel junction from a student project for handrail systems illustrates the ability of hydroforming to create a complex form that changes from one diameter to another through a complex curve. This could otherwise only be made using conventional forming techniques that would then need to be welded together.

**1  An example of the tooling and the die cavity into which the metal is placed.**

**2  Semi-finished hydroformed components.**

**Volumes of production**

High production volumes.

**Unit price vs capital investment**

Considerable investment in tooling required, but being able to produce components as single parts, rather than as multiple parts joined together, should help to reduce the price per unit.

**Speed**

In a highly automated factory setting, it is possible to achieve production cycle times of 20–30 seconds for a small part, even in a workflow set-up where parts are positioned and connected inside the die.

**Surface**

In general, hydroforming does not have much of an effect on the surfaces of materials. It does, however, leave small scratches and marks at the ends of a work piece from the clamps that seal the ends, but these are normally trimmed off.

**Types/complexity of shape**

Tubular materials can be made to bulge into quite elaborate forms. Examples of this include t-sections, which would otherwise need to be made by joining multiple components.

**Scale**

The bigger the part, the more pressure is needed for forming, which in turn requires a heavier mould to contain the powerful forces involved in this process. Some large car parts, including bonnets, can be made with hydroforming, although it would be difficult to manage pieces that were much larger than this.

**Tolerances**

Because of the die, the process allows the part to be controlled during forming to prevent wrinkling or tearing.

**Relevant materials**

Any metal with reasonably elastic properties that can take the high levels of tension involved, including high-grade steel and heat-treatable aluminium.

**Typical products**

Bicycle frames, bellows, t-sections and a variety of structural automobile components, including floor pans, van body sides and roof panels.

**Similar methods**

Inflating metal (p.62) and superforming aluminium (p.56).

**Further information**

www.hydroforming.net

http://salzgitter.westsachsen.de

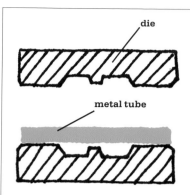

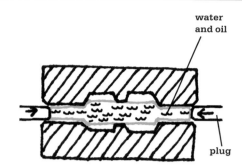

1  In tube forming, the metal tube is inserted into a two-part die and sealed at either end, with only one opening that allows the liquid to be fed in.

2  A water and oil solution is used to fill the tube and a pressure of up to 15,000 psi is applied by inserting plugs at either end of the tube, forcing the water to 'fill-out' the tube until it conforms to the die cavity.

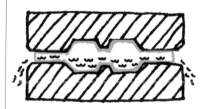

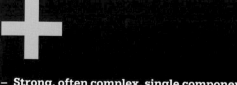

3  The solution is emptied from the filled-out tube.

4  The final, hollow part is removed.

**+**

- Strong, often complex, single components due to the elimination of joints.

- Potential for parts with lower weight but with high strength.

- Ability to reduce multiple components and joins into one complex part.

**—**

- High tooling investment needed.

- Limited number of companies offering the process.

# Backward Impact Extrusion
## AKA Indirect Extrusion

Impact extrusion is a cold process for forming metals that marries forging (see p.169) with extrusion (see p.78). In a nutshell, backward impact extrusion is a method of forming hollow metal parts by striking a metal billet (or disc), which is confined within a cylindrical or square die, so hard that the metal is forced upwards into the space between the 'hammer' (or punch) and the die. The gap between the punch and the inside of the die determines the wall thickness of the final component.

There are in fact two types of impact extrusion, forward extrusion and backward extrusion. Backward (or indirect) extrusion is used to make hollow shapes, because the punch is solid and thrusts the material around itself into the space between itself and the die.

| Product | Sigg drinks bottle |
| --- | --- |
| Materials | aluminium |
| Manufacturer | Sigg |
| Country | Switzerland |
| Date | range brought to market 1998 |

This cut-away of the famous Sigg container shows the thin walls and the typical shapes that are a feature of impact extrusion.

The other sort of impact extrusion, forward (or direct) extrusion, can only produce solid sections. In this instance the space between the punch and the die is too small to allow metal to wrap itself around the punch. Instead, the metal is hammered downwards into a die forming a straightforward solid shape. Nevertheless, these processes can also be combined in a single operation, where the repeated action of the punch pushes material both upwards (to form a hollow top) and downwards (to make a solid, shaped base).

Designs that require outward tapering may need some post forming after extrusion, and any threaded sections, such as the bottle neck, are also added after forming.

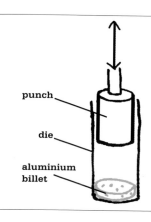

1 The aluminium billet, which is placed on the die.

2 The cylinder created by the action of the punch using backward extrusion.

3 Tapering is added by a secondary process.

4 With the threading at the neck added, this is now recognisable as a Sigg bottle.

punch
die
aluminium billet

1 An aluminium billet is placed in the die.

2 The die is punched with the impact forcing the material upwards into the space between the 'hammer' and the cylinder.

### Volumes of production

Impact extrusion is a high-volume production method. Depending on the size of the component, minimum quantities range from 3,000 upwards.

### Unit price vs capital investment

Surprisingly, tooling is not as expensive as you might expect for a process that is used for high volumes, but the speed with which it turns out products means that it requires a large minimum order. Unit costs are very low.

### Speed

The famous one-litre Sigg drinks bottles (pictured) are made at a rate of 28 per minute.

### Surface

Offers a reasonably high degree of surface finish.

### Types/complexity of shape

It is possible to produce thin- or thick-walled containers using backward impact extrusion, either cylindrical or square, that are closed at one end. (The forward process produces solid sections from solid rods of different shapes and sizes.) Both methods are best suited to symmetrical shapes. There are also certain guidelines regarding the ideal proportion of length and width, but you should consult your manufacturer, as these will depend on the material being used.

### Scale

Suitable for parts weighing from a few grams up to approximately 1 kilogram.

### Tolerances

High degrees of tolerance achievable by backward impact extrusion. (Obviously, forward impact extrusion offers greater tolerances because the final object is solid.)

### Relevant materials

Aluminium, magnesium, zinc, lead, copper and low-alloy steels.

### Typical products

Backward extrusion is a popular method for forming drinks and food cans, aerosol cans and similar containers. Forward and backward extrusion are used together to make such items as ratchet heads.

### Similar methods

Forging (p.169) and extrusion (p.78).

### Further information

www.mpma.org.uk
www.sigg.ch
www.aluminium.org

---

- Produces cost-effective shells in a variety of square and cylindrical cross-sectional shapes.

- Removes the issue of joints by producing components with a uniform, seamless wall.

- Inexpensive tooling compared with other high-volume processes.

---

- The final component is limited in length to the length of the punch needed to strike the billet.

- Only suited to parts where the length of the part is greater than four times the diameter.

- Post forming is required to add tapers or threads.

- Subject to the limitations of the die.

# Moulding Paper Pulp
## including rough pulp moulding and thermoforming

Paper is one of the most efficiently collected and recycled materials of the modern age. Much of what is collected is converted into pulp to make new products for a variety of industries, though these are usually simple sheets or packaging. However, it is the moulding of paper pulp using highly unusual mass-production technology that makes it particularly noteworthy.

The manufacture of moulded paper products is based on two methods: the conventional rough (or industrial) pulp process and a thermoforming process. Both methods begin by soaking the collected paper in water in a giant

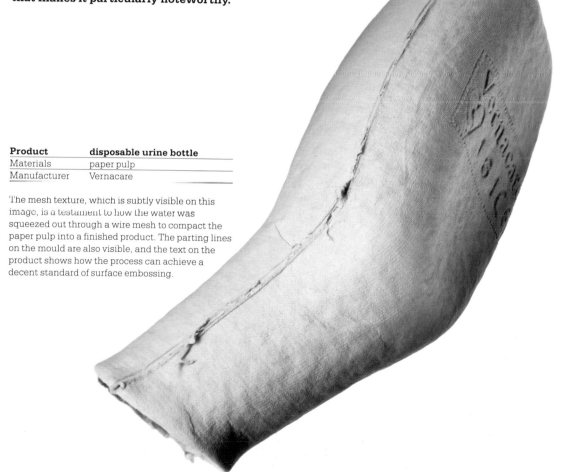

| Product | disposable urine bottle |
|---|---|
| Materials | paper pulp |
| Manufacturer | Vernacare |

The mesh texture, which is subtly visible on this image, is a testament to how the water was squeezed out through a wire mesh to compact the paper pulp into a finished product. The parting lines on the mould are also visible, and the text on the product shows how the process can achieve a decent standard of surface embossing.

### Volumes of production

Due to the high cost of tooling and the speed at which parts can be made, both rough pulp moulding and thermoforming require high volumes of production. Minimum runs of two days (about 50,000 pieces) are generally required.

### Unit price vs capital investment

Tooling costs and set-up times are high. The two methods have different tooling requirements; the thermoforming method costs approximately twice as much as the raw method.

### Speed

Thickness, and the amount of paper that needs to be dried, determine the speed. As a guide, the moulded inserts for four mobile-phone boxes take about a minute to produce. This is based on a multiple impression, meaning four components are moulded at the same time. These four different moulds can therefore produce 960 units per hour.

### Surface

Just think of a paper egg box to get a sense of that uniquely soft, warm, biscuity surface. The rough pulp process produces one rough side, picking up an impression from the wire mesh, and a smooth surface created by the polished aluminium, or plastic, face of the mould.

### Types/complexity of shape

Some fairly complex patterns can be moulded, but large draw angles need to be allowed for; forget any complex three-dimensional detailing.

### Scale

Standard production allows for up to 1,500 by 400 millimetre areas – however, some manufacturers can sustain sizes up to 2.4 metres long.

### Tolerances

Tolerances vary depending on the specific process. Tolerances of ± 0.5–1 millimetre are achievable using the thermoforming method. For the rough pulp process, ± 2–3 millimetres is achievable.

### Relevant materials

The raw materials come from two main sources: newsprint and cardboard. The choice of material depends on the final product and the strength that is required. For strong packaging that needs to satisfy drop-test requirements (used, for example, for mobile phones, PDAs and cameras), the long fibres found in cardboard provide the best solution.

### Typical products

Conventional rough pulp is used to make wine packs and industrial packaging. The thermoforming process is used to produce more sophisticated products such as mobile-phone packaging.

### Similar methods

None.

### Further information

www.huhtamaki.com
www.mouldedpaper.com
www.paperpulpsolutions.co.uk
www.vaccari.co.uk
www.vernacare.com

tank, with the proportions of paper and water based on the level of consistency needed to achieve the particular end product (typically, the amount of paper can be as low as 1 per cent). The resulting grey mixture is churned with a blade to produce the moulding compound of 'paper mush'.

Unlike most other material moulding methods, which involve the mould being stationary, the aluminium or plastic female moulds used in moulding paper pulp (which have draining holes all over them) are submerged in tanks of liquid paper pulp. The moulds are covered with mesh or gauze, which allows the water to drain out, hence the typical mesh impression that you can see on, for example, a standard egg box. A male mould is then used to compress the pulp, and a vacuum draws the water out of the mould, sucking the fibres firmly into the mould. At this point the whole thing is dried, thus forming the final product.

As well as using heat, as its name suggests, the thermoforming process involves the use of transfers and presses. After moulding, the component is picked up by a transfer, which is the negative shape of the component, and carried to a heated press that forms the final shape. It offers several advantages, including better quality surface finish but is more costly to set up.

– Uses recycled and recyclable material.
– Produces lightweight parts.

– Requires large production volumes.
– Only suitable for use with a limited range of materials.

# Contact Moulding
## including hand lay-up and spray lay-up moulding, vacuum-bag and pressure-bag forming

Contact moulding is a method of forming composites by taking plastic reinforcement fibres, layering them, then applying liquid resin over the top to create a hard shell. In its simplest form – the traditional hand lay-up method – the reinforcements are laid over a mould before the liquid resin is brushed or sprayed into it. If you have ever repaired a dent or hole in an old car or boat you will probably have used a simple version of this process. In industry, it is a process for producing large-scale mouldings in composite materials, and it is one of the most frequent methods of combining various types of reinforcement fibre with thermoset resins.

The open-form moulds used in hand lay-up can be made from any material, but wood, plastic or cement are the most common. The reinforcement fibres are generally glass or carbon, but other materials, including natural fibres, can be used. A resin is then applied with a brush or by spraying, before rollers are used to squash and to distribute the mixture evenly in the mould. The spray-up method is used when larger areas are involved, using short, chopped fibres that are incorporated into the resin before spraying. In both cases, the thickness of the part is controlled by the number of layers that are applied.

Vacuum-bag and pressure-bag forming are variations of the hand lay-up and spray lay-up methods for forming composites, but they give the moulding finer detail and greater strength. The procedure is similar for both variants: in the pressure-bag method, once the materials have been laid over the mould, a flexible bag made of rubber is placed over them and subjected to pressure by clamping it, which compacts the materials, squeezing the resin and reinforcement

- The use of reinforcing fibres results in high strength.
- Other performance additives, such as flame-retardants, can easily be incorporated.
- Versatile in terms of shape and size.
- Allows thick sections to be produced.

- Quite a labour-intensive process.
- Requires good ventilation due to the resins.
- Other composite-forming methods (such as filament winding, see p.140) offer much higher density and strength-to-weight ratios.

together; with the vacuum-bag method, the part is cured inside a bag from which the air has been sucked out, forcing the materials together.

With vacuum-bag forming it is possible to achieve similar results to those that you find with autoclave moulding (see p.138) but without the need for a pressure chamber. Compared with the hand and spray lay-up methods, both vacuum-bag and pressure-bag forming result in higher fibre content and density because of the use of a vacuum or pressure, which also limits the amount of potentially harmful vapour to a minimum.

### Volumes of production

Because of the labour involved in all these methods, the process is always slow. However, the nature of the spray-up method makes it faster than the hand lay-up process.

### Unit price vs capital investment

Tooling can be inexpensive, for all of these methods, but the time taken to form parts makes them expensive to mass-produce as a high-volume process.

### Speed

Depends on the type of hand lay-up technique and obviously the size of the moulding. Spray lay-up is faster, but since the areas are larger, unit speed will not necessarily be quicker.

### Surface

On the reverse of mouldings made with this type of method you will find the familiar fibrous texture of the reinforcement. Gel coats, which are coatings that do not contain reinforcement, can be applied to the mould to enhance the surface finish of components. Other thermoformed skins can be applied in a secondary process for a superior surface. The nature of the vacuum-bag and pressure-bag methods allows for a much greater degree of surface detail.

### Types/complexity of shape

All methods are limited to open shapes with fairly thin cross-sections. Only slight undercuts are possible, depending on how far the component can be flexed when removing it from the mould.

### Scale

As big as you want. Hand lay-up allows a much thicker wall thickness to be built up than spray lay-up, which reaches its maximum at about 15 millimetres. The scale of components using the bag methods is limited only by the size of the bags.

### Tolerances

Shrinkage will occur, so tolerances are hard to control for all methods.

### Relevant materials

Reinforcement materials include advanced fibres such as carbon, aramid and glass, but natural materials such as jute and cotton can also be used. Polyester is the most widely used thermosetting resin; others include epoxy, phenolic resin and silicone. Thermoplastics are also used, but they are far less cost-effective.

### Typical products

General glass-reinforced plastic (GRP) items such as boat hulls, car panels, furniture, bath tubs, shower trays and cheap seats on the decks of small Greek ferries.

### Similar methods

Transfer moulding (p.158) can achieve a similar strength. Gas-assisted injection moulding (p.183) and reaction injection moulding (p.181) can be used to create large parts, but without the strength. Other alternatives include vacuum infusion (VIP) (p.136), filament winding (p.140) and autoclave moulding (p.138).

### Further information

www.compositetek.com
www.netcomposites.com
www.compositesone.com
www.composites-by-design.com
www.fiberset.com

# Vacuum Infusion Process (VIP)

The vacuum infusion process (VIP) is a method of forming composites that achieves density and strength in the end product by sucking the resin and reinforcement fibres together into a dense, solid mass. In essence, it is an advanced form of contact moulding (see p.134) and, compared with similar techniques for forming composites, it is a clean and highly effective process through which the two main ingredients can be combined in a single step.

In traditional hand lay-up methods in contact moulding, the reinforcing fibres are laid over a mould before the liquid resin is brushed or sprayed into it. In the VIP process, the dry parts of the material are stacked up over a mould. This is then covered with a flexible sheet and a seal is formed between the sheet and the mould. The air is pumped out from inside, forming a vacuum, and the liquid polymer resin is then fed into the fibres. The action of the vacuum means that the resin thoroughly impregnates the dry material, which gives the final component its density and strength.

1  A boat hull being covered in a flexible plastic sheet, ready to be sealed prior to the application of a vacuum.

2  The sheet is inspected to make sure it is completely sealed.

3  The vacuum pumps that suck the air from between the sheet and the hull.

**Volumes of production**

This is a slow production method that relies on the luxury of a fairly long set-up time to build the part.

**Unit price vs capital investment**

VIP can be used in a small workshop with basic equipment, which can be purchased from various suppliers. However, it requires a lot of trial and error, and you may suffer a high failure rate.

**Speed**

Slow.

**Surface**

Gel coats can be applied to provide the parts with a high surface finish.

**Types/complexity of shape**

A common application for VIP is in the manufacture of boat hulls, which should give you an idea of the level of its complexity and its scale.

**Scale**

The process is suited to large parts. It is difficult to make anything smaller than around 300 by 300 millimetres, because the fibre needs to be draped over or inside the mould.

**Tolerances**

Not the kind of process for high tolerances.

**Relevant materials**

As in any plastic composite method, typical resins used are polyester, vinyl ester and epoxy, combined with reinforcements such as fibreglass, aramids and graphite.

**Typical products**

Propellers, marine components and equipment such as a stretcher used in rescue operations, which features an aluminium frame overmoulded with a vacuum-infused composite.

**Similar methods**

Contact moulding (p.134), transfer moulding (p.158) and autoclave moulding (p.138).

**Further information**

www.resininfusion.com

www.reichhold.com

www.epoxi.com/application/infusion.asp

- Economical use of resin due to the efficient ratio of fibre to resin.

- Clean.

- Eliminates air pockets.

- Higher strength-to-weight ratios than contact moulding (see p.134).

- Complicated set-up.

- High degree of trial and error.

- High failure rate.

# Autoclave Moulding

Advanced composite materials have applications across a range of industries, from premium branded sports products to engineering components. These materials offer superior strength in a lightweight moulding. However, the combination of the two distinctly different ingredients (various fibres and polymer resins) in advanced composites provides manufacturers with a challenge. They must find new ways to bring these raw materials together in a cost-effective manner that is suited to industrial production. The use of heat and pressure is a  very common elements within manufacturing. In autoclave moulding the combination is used to compact the raw materials together to offer the highest level of strength.

Autoclave moulding is a modified form of pressure-bag forming (see contact moulding p.134) – the composite is formed in what is essentially a pressure cooker. As a result of the applied pressure, it is one of the methods of forming advanced composite components with particularly high density. The process begins with the application of reinforcing fibres and resin onto a mould, which can be achieved through a variety of methods, such as hand or spray lay-up techniques (see contact moulding, p.134). A flexible bag is then placed, a little bit like a duvet, over the surface and the whole thing is placed in an autoclave (a sealed chamber), where heat and between 50 and 200 psi of pressure are applied, forcing the bag to squeeze itself into, or around, the mould, compressing the resin and fibres together. This forces out any potential air gaps and allows for a relatively fast curing time, compared with hand or spray lay-up. It is the squeezing together of materials under pressure, with the application of heat, that gives the final component a very high density.

## Volumes of production
Batch production to medium-level production.

## Unit price vs capital investment
Moulds can be manufactured from a range of materials, including modelling clay, which allows reasonably cheap tooling to be produced for short-batch production.

## Speed
Although the laying together of the resin and reinforcement can be automated, the process requires manual labour and the material must pass through a number of stages. The time the material spends in the autoclave can be up to 15 hours.

## Surface
Gel coats are sometimes used on the surface of the mould to provide a higher quality surface finish. Without this gel, the surface would have a fibrous texture.

## Types/complexity of shape
Although the process is versatile in terms of being adaptable to different shaped moulds, it is nevertheless limited to fairly simple shapes.

## Scale
Part sizes are only limited by the size of the autoclave.

## Tolerances
Shrinkage does occur, so tolerances are hard to control.

## Relevant materials
Suited to various advanced fibres, such as carbon fibre, and thermoset polymers.

## Typical products
Widely used in the aerospace industry to fabricate high strength-to-weight ratio parts for aircraft, spacecraft and missile nose cones.

## Similar methods
All forms of contact moulding (p.134), the vacuum infusion process (VIP) (p.136) and filament winding (p.140).

## Further information
www.netcomposites.com

- Increased density, faster cure times and void-free mouldings compared with moulding methods that use neither heat nor pressure.

- Potential for moulded-in colour.

- Suitable only for making hollow parts that have thick, dense walls.

# Filament Winding

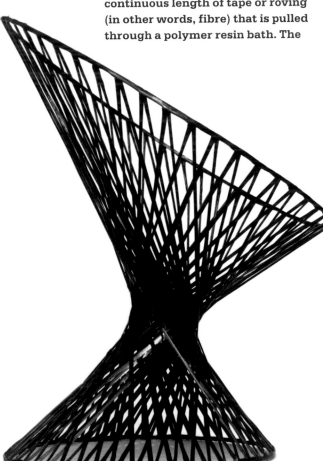

Imagine impregnating the thread on a cotton reel with resin and then being able to pull the wound thread off its reel to form a rigid plastic cylindrical part: this is the essence of filament winding.

In filament winding, a reinforcement fibre combined with a polymer resin is used to form strong, hollow composites. It involves a continuous length of tape or roving (in other words, fibre) that is pulled through a polymer resin bath. The sticky fibre is wound over a pre-formed mandrel in a process that is allowed to continue until the required thickness of material is built up. The shape of the mandrel determines the internal dimensions of the finished product. If the end product is likely to be used in pressurised conditions, the mandrel may be left inside the winding to add strength.

There are various forms of filament winding that differ only in the configuration of the winding. These include circumferencial winding, where the threads are wound in parallel like the cotton thread on a spool; helical winding, where the threads are wound at an angle to the spool (which gives a woven surface pattern that is instantly recognizable); and polar winding, where the threads are run almost horizontally to the axis of the spool.

| Product | spun carbon chair |
|---|---|
| Designer | Mathias Bengtsson |
| Materials | carbon fibre and polymer resin |
| Country | UK |
| Date | 2003 |

This chair is made using a helical winding technique, though the desired effect is more gappy than is usual for components made from filament winding. This highly decorative spun structure firmly establishes filament winding – a process most often associated with engineering composites – as a design application.

1  Three composite tubes being formed on a three-spindle filament-winding machine.

2  The yellow control arm feeds the resin-impregnated fibres onto the tube-shaped mandrel. (The resin bath is out of frame.)

3  The helical winding pattern of the fibres is clearly visible.

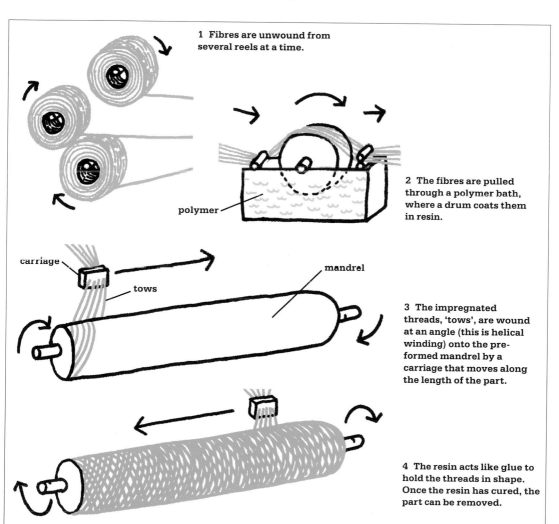

1  Fibres are unwound from several reels at a time.

2  The fibres are pulled through a polymer bath, where a drum coats them in resin.

polymer

carriage

tows

mandrel

3  The impregnated threads, 'tows', are wound at an angle (this is helical winding) onto the pre-formed mandrel by a carriage that moves along the length of the part.

4  The resin acts like glue to hold the threads in shape. Once the resin has cured, the part can be removed.

### Volumes of production

Equally suited to one-off and high-volume production. Economical mass-production starts at approximately 5,000 units and can range up to hundreds of thousands of units.

### Unit price vs capital investment

Foam tooling can be used for small runs or one-off production, as can existing aluminium bar stock, so costs can be kept down.

### Speed

The speed is dependent on the shape and desired wall thickness of the final component. However, by using a 'prepreg' system, where the fibres are pre-coated in resin, the process eliminates the need for a resin bath. Speed is also affected by the number of 'tows' of fibre that are used, so that multiple tows result in a faster covering of the mandrel.

### Surface

The internal surface depends on the finish on the mandrel, while the external surface can be finished in a number of ways, including with machining.

### Types/complexity of shape

Produces very strong, thin- or thick-walled hollow components, including asymmetrical shapes.

### Scale

Machines can be built to produce filament windings to a massive scale. An all-plastic, 396 metre-long motor case for a NASA rocket with a 53 metre diameter was produced in the 1960s.

### Tolerances

Tolerance is controlled by the internal diameter, which is determined by the size of the mandrel.

### Relevant materials

Generally used to reinforce thermosetting plastic with glass or carbon fibre.

### Typical products

This is a process that is often used for closed-pressure vessels such as aeronautical components, tanks and rocket-motor housings. Because of the high strength-to-weight ratio of these parts, they are used as 'stealth' materials to replace metals in military hardware. The process is also used for its more decorative capabilities in expensive 'designer' pens made from composite materials, as well as in the chair (pictured).

### Similar methods

Pultrusion (p.81 and hand or spray lay-up (see contact moulding, p.134).

### Further information

www.ctgltd.co.uk
www.vetrotexeurope.com
www.composites-proc-assoc.co.uk
www.acmanet.org

**+**

– **Produces components with a very high strength-to-weight ratio.**

**−**

– **Filament-wound components will always have a woven surface pattern unless they are post-finished.**

# Centrifugal Casting
including true- and semi-centrifugal casting, and centrifuging

Centrifugal casting is a process that is based on a specific use of gravity. The same force that is at work when lettuce leaves are spun in a salad spinner, or when people are rotated in a waltzer at the funfair, is employed to thrust a heated liquid material horizontally against the inside of a mould. Once the liquid has cooled, the finished part is taken out of the mould. In industrial manufacturing, centrifugal casting is most often used to make large-scale metal cylinders that require specific surface properties within the metal component.

Centrifugal casting for metals can be broken down into three main variants: true centrifugal casting, semi-centrifugal casting and centrifuging. As you may well have guessed, each process uses a centrifugal force to throw molten metal against the inside wall of a mould to produce a variety of shapes.

True centrifugal casting is used to make pipes and tubes, and it involves molten metal being poured into a rotating cylindrical mould. The mould defines the outside surface of the final component, while the wall thickness of the final tube or pipe is determined by the amount of material that is poured in. This type of casting solves one of the problems traditionally associated with metal, because the outer surface of the component is of such a fine grain that it is resistant to atmospheric corrosion (which is a common issue with pipes), while the internal diameter is rougher, with more impurities.

In semi-centrifugal casting, either permanent or disposable moulds are employed for making symmetrical shapes such as wheels and nozzles. It involves a vertical spindle around which the mould is held, like a spinning top. It also involves a slower rotation than true centrifugal casting and parts can be 'stacked' – in other words, more than one part can be made at a time because multiple moulds can be attached to the spindle. Because the material nearest the centre (that is, nearest the spindle) rotates at a slower rate than the material furthest away, small air pockets can occur in the component.

Centrifuging is similar to semi-centrifugal casting in as much as the spinning occurs around a vertical spindle, but it is used to produce small multiple components. The metal is forced into the various mould cavities (which are only a short distance from the spindle) to produce fine details.

### Volumes of production

From a relatively simple set-up in a workshop for making jewellery, to large-scale industrial production, these are processes that can be used for batch-rather than mass-production.

### Unit price vs capital investment

Depending on the specific type of production, different materials can be used for the moulds. Low-cost graphite moulds can be used for small production runs (up to about 60 pieces), while more expensive permanent steel moulds are used for larger runs of, perhaps, several hundred.

### Speed

Slow, but it varies depending on the material that is used and the size, shape and desired wall thickness of the part.

### Surface

True centrifugal casting produces an outer surface of fine-grain quality. Due to the slower rotation speed of semi-centrifugal casting, the forces in the centre of the casting are small, so gaps and porosity generally occur that need to be machined away after forming. Centrifuging enables fine details to be produced.

### Types/complexity of shape

True centrifugal casting produces only tubular shapes. Semi-centrifugal casting produces parts that are axisymmetric (that is, symmetrical around the vertical spindle) in shape only. Centrifuging is more versatile, and can be used produce more complex shapes.

### Scale

True centrifugal casting can be used to form massive tubes up to 3 metres in diameter and 15 metres long. Wall thickness can be between 3 and 125 millimetres. Semi-centrifugal casting and centrifuging produce smaller parts.

### Tolerances

The tolerances can be as good as 0.5 millimetres on the outer diameter when using metal moulds.

### Relevant materials

Most materials that can be cast by other methods, including iron, carbon steels, stainless steels, bronze, brasses and alloys of aluminium, copper and nickel. Two materials can be cast simultaneously by introducing a second material during the process. Glass and plastics can also be used.

### Typical products

The casting of metals is based in heavy industry, where it is used for hollow parts with large diameters. Typical parts made by true centrifugal casting are pipes for the oil and chemical industries, and water-supply components. The process is also used in the production of poles for lighting and other street furniture. Semi-centrifugal casting produces axisymmetric parts, such as storage containers for wine and milk, boilers, pressure vessels, flywheels and cylinder liners. On a smaller scale, jewellers use centrifuging for more modestly sized metal and plastic parts.

### Similar methods

Rotational moulding (p.119), although in centrifugal casting the mould is rotated at much higher speeds. Due to the limited types of shape that centrifugal casting produces, it is difficult to compare it with other casting methods.

### Further information

www.sgva.com/fabrication_
    processes/rna_centrif.htm
www.acipco.com
www.jtprice.fsnet.co.uk

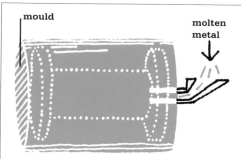

mould

molten
metal

1  Molten metal is poured into a sealed mould.

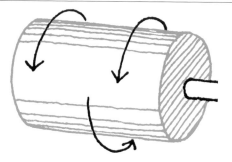

2  The mould is rotated around its axis at between 300 and 3,000 rpm.

3  The rotating action of the mould throws the metal against the inside walls of the mould. The quantity of metal determines the wall thickness of the final component.

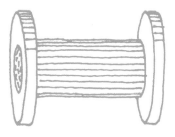

4  The finished component, removed from the mould.

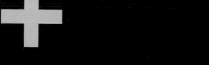

**+**

- Parts can be produced with good mechanical properties in all directions, because the process results in non-directional grain orientation.

- The strength of centrifugal castings is close to that of wrought metal.

- With true centrifugal casting, the outer surface has a fine grain, which makes it more resistant to corrosion.

- Can achieve economical production over short runs.

**–**

- Limited production base.
- Limited shapes achievable.

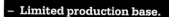

# Electroforming

This process has changed very little since the early nineteenth century, when simple electroplating – a way of plating metals from their salts – was developed out of the initial work of British scientist Sir Humphry Davy on passing currents through electrolytes. Situated somewhere between a surface coating and a form-making technique, electroforming is a fairly unusual process. It is perhaps best explained by way of comparing it to growing a 'skin' over a shape. The 'skin' ultimately becomes the final component once it is lifted off the mould. Essentially, it is a step on from electroplating, in which the layer of metal acts only as a coating for the original shape.

Electroforming is based on the electro-depositing of metal onto moulds. The shape that would, in simple electroplating, be coated (the cathode), in electroforming becomes a mould onto which the metalising source (the anode) is grown, in a solution of electrolyte. An electrical current forces metal ions from the anode onto the cathode. Once a sufficient build-up of metal has been achieved – and this is where it differs radically from electroplating – the component is separated from the mould. The mould does not necessarily have to be made from metals – it can be made from any non-conductive material, which can be coated with a conductive outside layer before plating.

The usefulness of electroforming lies in the fact that intricate flat and three-dimensional patterns can be easily reproduced without the need for expensive tooling, because the detail is created on the mould. The process is unique in that it creates a uniformly thin layer of material around the mould, unlike press forming (see metal cutting p.51) and sheet-metal forming (see p.44), which stretches the metal and, in so doing, leaves it an uneven thickness.

1  A negative mould of the part to be produced is placed in a bath of electrolyte solution with the base metal. A current is then applied, which forces ions from the base metal onto the mould to build up a layer of metal.

2  When a sufficient build-up of metal has been achieved, the component is separated from the mould.

### Volumes of production

Due to the length of time it takes to load moulds into the tank and produce the build-up of metal, this is not a process for high-volume or rapid production.

### Unit price vs capital investment

This is an economical way of reproducing designs that are intricately patterned without needing a large investment in tooling. The cost of electroforming is partly determined by the amount of metal used, so the final unit price will depend on the surface area of the mould and the thickness of the deposited metal.

### Speed

Slow, but depends on the amount of metal to be deposited.

### Surface

Due to the nature of this process (the fact that it uses a mould and parts are built up gradually from tiny ions), the surface pattern can be highly intricate.

### Types/complexity of shape

An ideal process for making multiple units of complex, highly decorative shapes. Making the mould from materials such as wax, which can be melted out after electroforming, means undercuts are possible.

### Scale

The only limitation is the size of the electrolyte bath that holds the mould.

### Tolerances

Unlike other metal-forming techniques, electroforming can produce extremely high tolerances, where the build-up of material is exactly the same anywhere on the part. This is unlike when a piece of metal is bent, a process that creates thick areas of material in corners.

### Relevant materials

Nickel, gold, copper, alloys such as nickel-cobalt and other electroplateable alloys.

### Typical products

A great deal of highly decorated, hollow Victorian silver tableware was produced using the technique. Today, it is still used for highly detailed silverware, but it is also used for technical laboratory apparatus and in musical instruments – a brass horn, for example.

### Similar methods

Simple electroplating, and as part of the micro-moulding with electroforming process (see p.222).

### Further information

www.acsf.org
www.drc.com/metrigraphics
  /electroforming
www.ajtuckco.com/eformpro
www.finishing.com
www.precisionmicro.com

- Excellent definition in detailing.
- Generates a uniform thickness of metal.
- Low tooling costs.
- An easy way to replicate existing products.
- High tolerance.

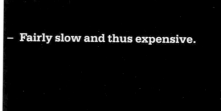

- Fairly slow and thus expensive.

# 5: Into Solid

# The transformation of a material into a solid state

This chapter deals principally with a group of processes that fall within the realm of 'powder metallurgy'. This term no longer adequately describes the advanced and wide-ranging technology that exists, nor the materials. The advanced materials that are used are not always in powder form, and they include ceramics and plastics as well as metals. Processes that in the simplest terms were based on compacting metal powders into shape and then sintering the 'green' component to fuse the tiny particles together, can now be applied to many different (though mostly particulate) materials. The one exception to the powder metallurgy classification is forging, which involves transformation of an object from one solid state to another.

# Sintering
## including pressure-less, pressure and spark sintering, die-pressing and sintering

Sintering (a derivative of the word 'cinder') was traditionally associated with the manufacture of ceramic objects. The term is now, however, also widely used in the much larger manufacturing area of powder metallurgy. Essentially, sintering involves heating a particulate material to just below its melting point until the particles fuse together.

Various forms of sintering exist in the metals, plastics, glass and ceramics industries. Pressure-less sintering involves a powder being placed in a mould that is heated and vibrated, and then sintered. Pressure sintering involves powder being placed in a mould, vibrated and then heated, with pressure applied either mechanically or hydraulically. In spark sintering, a pulsed current passes through the mould into the powder, generating heat internally (in contrast to the above methods, where heat is applied). Die-pressing and sintering is used predominantly for ceramic or metal powders. In this process, the powder is first die-pressed into a 'green' state of the required form. This is then heated so that the particles sinter, or, in other words, fuse together.

Sintering is used to achieve high density in parts made from materials with high melting points, such as tungsten and Teflon where low porosity is needed. One of the characteristics of sintered parts, however, is that the porosity of the final component can be controlled, especially with certain materials. The porosity of some materials even after sintering can have its advantages: bronze, for example, is often used as a material for bearings, since its porosity allows lubricants to flow through. An alternative method, which eliminates porosity, is hot isostatic pressing (HIP) (see p.152).

There is also an advanced form, selective laser sintering (SLS) (see p.224), in which the application of heat is highly controlled. This method is used for rapid prototyping.

### Volumes of production

Can be used for fairly low production volumes as well as for metal injection-moulded parts (see p.192), which require a minimum of 10,000 units.

### Unit price vs capital investment

Tooling costs range from low to high, depending on the specific process. The nature of the process also makes it highly efficient because there is no wasted material.

### Speed

This varies considerably depending on the material and the method used. For example, once compacted into shape, in the pressure-less method parts are put onto a continuous-belt furnace. Bronze typically needs 5 to 10 minutes at the centre of the furnace to sinter, while steel needs a minimum of 30 minutes.

### Surface

Although the finished parts can be porous, visually there is no difference in finish compared with, for example, a standard high-pressure die casting (see p.195) or metal-injection moulding. There is also a range of finishes that can be used on sintered parts, including electroplating, oil and chemical blackening, and varnishing.

### Types/complexity of shape

Not suited to thin-walled sections. Shapes must not have undercuts.

### Scale

Scale is limited to the size of the compacting press up to a maximum of 700 by 580 by 380 millimetres. Larger presses can produce approximately 2,000 tonnes of pressure, with parts requiring 50 tonnes per square inch.

### Tolerances

Due to problems with shrinkage (there is a reduction in volume because of the increase of density as material flows into voids), high tolerances are generally hard to obtain unless a part goes through a secondary pressing and compaction.

### Relevant materials

A variety of ceramics, glass, metals and plastic can be sintered.

### Typical products

One of the most interesting examples is the production of bearings, where the natural porosity produced by the process allows lubricants to flow through the actual bearings. Other common examples include hand tools, surgical tools, orthodontic brackets and golf clubs.

### Similar methods

Hot isostatic pressing (HIP) (p.152) and cold isostatic pressing (CIP) (p.154).

### Further information

www.mpif.org
www.cisp.psu.edu

- Suited to components with varying wall thicknesses.
- Efficient use of materials.
- Capable of forming materials that are difficult to deal with in other ways, especially very hard or brittle materials.
- Parts have good non-directional properties.
- Can produce complex forms.

- Requires a number of different stages.
- Difficult to achieve high tolerances due to the decrease in overall volume in sintered parts.

# Hot Isostatic Pressing (HIP)

Hot isostatic pressing (HIP) is one of the main processes for forming materials that fall under the umbrella term 'powder metallurgy' (a term that now also refers to other particulate materials, including ceramics and plastics). Heat and pressure, typically in the form of argon or nitrogen gas, are applied to powder resulting in parts with no porosity and high density, without the need for sintering (see p.150). The word 'isostatic' indicates that pressure is applied equally from all sides.

Essentially, the process involves powdered materials being placed inside a container which is subjected to high temperature and vacuum pressure to remove air and moisture from the powder. The resulting highly compacted component is uniformly and 100 per cent dense.

The process can be used either to form components from powder or to consolidate existing components. In the latter case, there is no need for a mould as the shape has already been formed. HIP is often used for castings that need to be made denser by eliminating porosity.

| Product | knife from the 'Kyotop' range |
|---|---|
| Designer | Yoshiyuki Matsui |
| Materials | zirconia ceramic |
| Manufacturer | Kyocera |
| Country | Japan |
| Date | 2000 |

The ceramic blade of this quality knife retains its sharpness well, and has the added benefit that ceramic does not impart any taste onto food. The visible pattern, known as the 'Sandgarden effect', is lasered onto the ceramic as a secondary process.

### Volumes of production

HIP is generally suitable only for medium-scale production quantities, typically less than 10,000 pieces.

### Unit price vs capital investment

The process requires large set-up costs with expensive components.

### Speed

Slow.

### Surface

It is possible to achieve very high surface quality with ceramics, but other materials may require subsequent machining and polishing.

### Types/complexity of shape

Simple to complex shapes are possible.

### Scale

HIP caters for a range of sizes, from components measured in millimetres to large-scale products up to several metres in length.

### Tolerances

Low

### Relevant materials

Most materials can be used, including plastics, but the ones that are employed most commonly are advanced ceramics and metal powders such as titanium, various steels and beryllium.

### Typical products

The cost of the operation limits its use to high-spec components that require high physical and mechanical properties, such as turbine-engine components and orthopaedic implants. In advanced ceramics, HIP is used to form zirconia knife blades, silicon nitride ball bearings and oil-well drilling bits made from tungsten carbide.

### Similar methods

Cold isostatic pressing (CIP) (p.154). There is also a sort of injection moulding that is suitable for ceramics.

### Further information

www.mpif.org
www.ceramics.org
www.aiphip.com
www.bodycote.com
http://hip.bodycote.com

---

**+**

- Produces parts of high density with no porosity.

- Because the process produces a uniform pressure, the microstructure of the final components is uniform, without weak areas.

- Capable of producing larger parts than is possible with other powder-metallurgy processes.

- Suitable for producing complex shapes.

- Provides an efficient use of material.

- Improves toughness and cracking resistance in advanced ceramics.

- Eliminates sintering (see p.150), which is a secondary process in other powder metallurgy-based methods of production.

---

**—**

- Costly set-up.

- Shrinkage can be problematic.

# Cold Isostatic Pressing (CIP)

The best way to sum up this process is to think of squeezing wet sand between your hands so that most of the water is forced out, leaving a fairly hard lump that resembles the inside of your hand. Although this sort of pressing can be done at elevated temperatures, cold isostatic pressing (CIP) is a method of forming ceramics or metal components at ambient temperatures from powders, and it involves the powder being placed in a flexible rubber bag, which squeezes around the mould when equal pressure is applied from all directions, compressing and compacting the powders into a uniform density. The process provides a uniformity of compaction around the entire component, unlike conventional forms of pressing, such as compression moulding (see p.158), which require two-part moulds.

The process is broken down into two types: wet bag and dry bag. In wet-bag pressing the rubber mould is placed inside a liquid, which, as you would expect, transmits the pressure from all directions. In dry-bag pressing, the pressure is exerted from fluid which is pumped through channels in the tooling.

| Product | spark plug |
|---|---|
| Materials | alumina ceramic |
| Manufacturer | Bosch |

The spark plug is a common product but it is made using a little-known process. The white alumina is the part that has been made using CIP.

## Wet-bag method

particulate material

rubber bag

isostatic pressure

A particulate material is placed in a rubber bag. Pressure is then applied, compressing and compacting the powder into a uniform density.

### Volumes of production

Dry-bag presses are typically automated from the powder-filling to the part-removal stage, but this is a low-volume production method used to produce parts in their thousands rather than tens of thousands.

### Unit price vs capital investment

Tooling can be expensive for large production runs, although existing tooling can be customised for short-batch production.

### Speed

The speed depends on the particular process – for example, in the wet-bag method the rubber mould is removed from the liquid after each cycle and refilled. The dry-bag method, however, has the bag as an integral part of the mould so it does not need to be removed, but is reused to form multiple parts.

### Surface

Depends on how complicated the component is. Simple forms will not need any further finishing.

### Types/complexity of shape

The wet and dry methods are suited to different complexities of shapes. The wet-bag method is used for complex components because of the flexible mould, which allows for easy removal of the component. It allows complex shapes to be produced, including undercuts and re-entrant angles such as collars and threads. The dry-bag presses are suited to simple shapes that can be easily removed from the moulds.

### Scale

The wet-bag method is suited to large shapes, while the dry-bag presses are suited to smaller components.

### Tolerances

± 0.25 millimetres or 2 per cent, whichever is greater.

### Relevant materials

Advanced ceramics and other refractory materials, titanium alloys and tool steels.

### Typical products

The process is suited to products that are used in harsh, aggressive environments, such as cutting tools, advanced ceramic components including carbides and refractory components. Other applications for pressed ceramics and metals include automotive cylinder-liners for aircraft and marine gas turbine components, corrosion-resistant components for petrochemical equipment and nuclear reactors, and medical implants. However, the most common product that is made by CIP is the spark plug.

### Similar methods

Hot isostatic pressing (HIP) (p.152). It is also possible to use injection moulding for ceramics.

### Further information

www.dynacer.com
www.mpif.org/designcenter/isostatic

– The main advantage of CIP over other powder metallurgy methods lies in its ability to produce parts with a uniform density, with predictable shrinkage rates on a larger scale.

– Low production rates.

# Compression Moulding

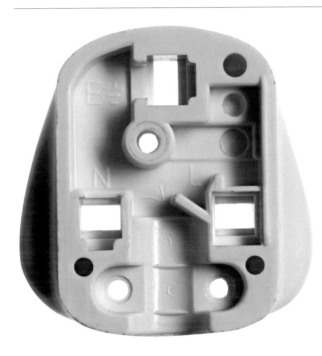

This process can be pressed into service for forming several different materials. On the one hand, it is used for producing ceramics, and on the other, it can be used to mould thermoset plastics (it was the original method for forming Bakelite), as well as fibre-based plastic composites.

To understand the basic principle of compression moulding, just think of children jamming their fists into lumps

| Product | electrical plug |
|---|---|
| Materials | phenol-formaldehyde plastic, also known as phenolic or Bakelite |
| Manufacturer | MK Electric |

A ubiquitous product that is an invaluable part of everyday life, but the process that lies behind it is frequently undervalued.

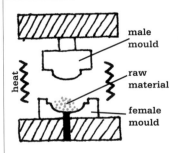

1  A two-part mould is heated and the granulated material (or sometimes a pre-form) is placed in the mould.

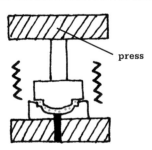

2  A press brings the lower and upper parts of the heated mould together, compressing the material into shape, the thickness of which is determined by the distance between the male and female parts.

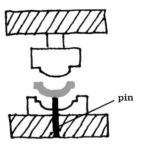

3  The moulds are separated and the formed component is ejected by pins.

of dough to create imprints. The elaborated industrial process uses granules as a starting point rather than solid material, and heated moulds to replace the fist. The two-part male and female moulds can be used to process anything from thick, solid shapes to thin-walled containers.

**Volumes of production**
Can be equally suitable for batch or high-volume production.

**Unit price vs capital investment**
In relation to other plastic-moulding methods (for example, injection moulding, see p.178), tooling costs are moderate while still maintaining a low unit price.

**Speed**
Speed is affected by how long the mould remains closed, which is determined by part size and material.

**Surface**
Good surface quality.

**Types/complexity of shape**
Compression moulding is often used for large plastic parts with thick wall sections, which can be more economically produced with this process than with injection moulding. The nature of shaping objects with a two-part, male/female mould makes the process suitable for simple forms with no undercuts, but it also means that parts can have variable wall thicknesses.

**Scale**
Generally used for small parts of approximately 300 millimetres in any direction.

**Tolerances**
Fair.

**Relevant materials**
Ceramics and thermoset plastics such as melamine and phenolics, and fibre composites and cork.

**Typical products**
Melamine kitchenware (bowls, cups and similar products) is often made with compression moulding. Other applications include electrical housings, switches and handles.

**Similar methods**
Hand and spray lay-up moulding (p.134) and transfer moulding (p.158). And, although more expensive, injection moulding (p.178) could also be considered.

**Further information**
www.bpf.co.uk
www.corkmasters.com
www.amorimsolutions.com

- Ideal for forming thermoset plastics.
- Ideal for producing parts that require large, thick-walled, solid sections.
- Allows for variable sections and wall thicknesses.

- Limited in terms of complexity of shapes, but good for producing flat shapes such as dinner plates.

# Transfer Moulding

An alternative to compression moulding (see p.156) and with some of the benefits of injection moulding (see p.178), transfer moulding is typically used to make large mouldings with varying wall thicknesses and fine surface detail.

| Product | body panels for a London bus |
|---|---|
| Materials | glass-filled thermoset plastic |

The exterior body panels on this type of bus have been made using transfer moulding. The easy flow of material through the mould cavity means that large components can be made without sacrificing control of the wall thickness.

The process involves a polymer resin being heated and loaded into a charger, where a plunger compresses the material. The heated material is then 'transferred' to a closed mould cavity. The defining characteristics of transfer moulding are this heating of the material before it is transferred, and the use of a closed mould. They allow the easy flow of the material through the cavity, which results in a finer degree of control over thin-walled sections and the ability to achieve fine detail on parts. Composite materials can be made by mixing fibres with the resin, or by laying the reinforcing fibres in the mould itself.

polymer resin — pump
air
catalyst material
mixing head
air vents
plunger
mould
fibres

A polymer resin is heated and loaded into a charger. Here a plunger compresses the material and 'transfers' it into a closed mould cavity.

## Volumes of production

Although traditionally associated with low-volume production, recent developments have allowed transfer moulding to evolve into a full-scale industrial process.

## Unit price vs capital investment

Because of the reasonably fast cycle times, transfer moulding suits high production runs, which confers the benefit of low unit costs but, as you would expect, entails high tooling costs

## Speed

This varies very much depending on the size of the part and the fibre content. Small parts can have cycle times as low as three minutes, while up to two hours is normal for large and complicated mouldings.

## Surface

A good surface finish is achievable similar to that produced by injection moulding (see p.178).

## Types/complexity of shape

Similar to injection moulding, but you should bear in mind that complex mouldings can increase production cycle times considerably.

## Scale

It is possible to achieve a much larger scale than with, for example, injection moulding. In one recent example, the Ford Motor Company was able to swap the entire 90-piece front end of the Ford Escort for a two-piece transfer-moulded assembly.

## Tolerances

Because the process involves the use of a closed mould, it achieves a greater tolerance than is possible with, for example, compression moulding (see p.156).

## Relevant materials

Most often used are thermoset plastics and composites.

## Typical products

Toilet seats, propeller blades and automotive components (such as the body panels for the bus, illustrated) are often made using transfer moulding.

## Similar methods

Compression moulding (p.156), although it has several drawbacks compared with transfer moulding, and injection moulding (p.178), which is not as well suited to forming composites. The vacuum infusion process (VIP) (p.136) can also be used for forming composites.

## Further information

www.hexcel.com
www.raytheonaircraft.com

**+**

- Reasonably fast production rates.
- Allows complex and intricate parts to be produced.
- Allows large components with varying, thin- and thick-walled sections to be produced.

**−**

- Inefficient use of materials due to excess material left in runners during the moulding process.
- Expensive tooling.

# Foam Moulding

Unlike many other plastic-processing methods, the production of expanded plastic foam requires the material – in the case of the chair illustrated here, expanded polypropylene (EPP) – to go through a pre-expansion process before it can be manufactured. It's a bit like preparing the ingredients before you embark on a recipe.

The raw material consists of tiny beads, which, before moulding, are expanded to 40 times their original size using pentane gas and steam. This causes the beads to boil, after which they are allowed to cool and stabilise. A partial vacuum is formed inside each bead, and the beads are then stored for several hours in order for the temperature and pressure inside them to equalise. The beads are reheated and steam is used to inject them into the mould and to fuse them together. (It is also possible to perform the initial expansion of the beads within the final mould, rather than injecting the already fused beads into the mould.) The mould itself is similar to a mould that might be used in injection moulding (see p.178), with a cavity to form the final component. This recipe for moulding plastics produces materials that are up to 98 per cent air.

Enzo Mari's design for the Seggiolina POP child's chair utilises these properties in a way that celebrates the material itself. This is in contrast to

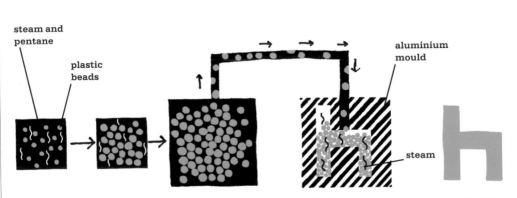

steam and pentane

plastic beads

aluminium mould

steam

1 The raw material of tiny spherical plastic beads is expanded to about 40 times its original size by the combined use of steam and pentane.

2 Once cooled, a partial vacuum is formed inside the beads, which are then left for approximately 12 hours to allow the pressure to equalise with the external environment.

3 The final stage involves the beads being reheated with steam, inside an aluminium mould.

4 Once cooled, the formed part is removed.

its more general applications, where it tends to be hidden away in a cardboard box or under upholstery.

As well as producing stand-alone components and products, various manufacturers have developed technology that enables expanded polypropylene to be moulded directly into the casings of other components, reducing assembly times and costs.

| Product | Seggiolina Pop chair |
|---|---|
| Designer | Enzo Mari |
| Materials | expanded polypropylene (EPP) |
| Manufacturer | Magis |
| Country | Italy |
| Date | 2004 |

The bright colours of the Seggiolina chair helps translate a traditionally industrial material and process into an intelligent, fun and lightweight product for children.

**Volumes of production**
High-volume production process.

**Unit price vs capital investment**
Aluminium tooling can be very expensive but produces highly cost-effective unit parts.

**Speed**
The moulding cycle times are typically 1 to 2 minutes, depending on the material.

**Surface**
The material can be coloured and printed with surface patterns, and graphics can be moulded into the surface. The surface is dependent on the density of the foam that you require, but all mouldings will have the textured foam finish that is typical of this type of material. It is also possible to produce different colour combinations within the same components, giving a mottled, multi-coloured effect.

**Types/complexity of shape**
Similar to the level of complexity that is possible with injection mouldings (see p.178), but with thicker and chunkier walls.

**Scale**
Foam moulding is a very versatile process that is capable of producing parts as small as 20 cubic millimetres up to blocks with a profile of 1 by 2 metres.

**Tolerances**
Tolerances vary a little between materials, but in general it is possible to work to an accuracy of about 2 per cent of the overall dimensions, with slightly higher figures for wall thicknesses.

**Relevant materials**
Expanded polystyrene (EPS), expanded polypropylene (EPP) and expanded polyethylene (EPE).

**Typical products**
Surfboards and bicycle helmets, packaging including fruit and vegetable trays, insulation blocks, head-impact protection in car headrests, bumper cores and steering-column fillers, as well as acoustic dampening.

**Similar methods**
Injection moulding (p.178) and reaction injection moulding (RIM) (p.181).

**Further information**
www.magismetoo.com
www.tuscarora.com
www.epsmolders.org
www.besto.nl

– **Very versatile in terms of scale and application.**

– **Improved structural properties.**

– **Reduced weight.**

– **Expensive tooling.**

# Foam Moulding into Plywood Shell

The constructional advantages and lightweight qualities of veneers were recognised by the makers of early aircraft, such as the Mosquito, and the structural use of thin veneers is nothing new in the manufacture of furniture. However, our interest in this engineered wood has now shifted to more innovative applications in furniture production.

The construction of one such example, the 'Laleggera' chair (pictured), reveals a reverse type of tailoring. Starting with the thin veneers, the chair is constructed in the same way that a child might assemble a model kit, with a set of net shapes that are glued together at the edges, leaving a hollow shell with no structural integrity. To provide structural integrity, the shell is then injected with a polyurethane foam that, when cured, becomes rigid. This is an adaptation of the more conventional type of foam moulding (see p.160), in which foam is injected through steam into an aluminium mould where it expands to form its own skin, and can then be removed from the mould.

The great feature of the 'Laleggera' range of furniture and the process developed by Alias is that it takes two highly uncommon materials and methods and brings them together to produce a new functional and aesthetic feature for furniture that is disarmingly lightweight.

| Product | chair from the 'Laleggera' range |
| --- | --- |
| Designer | Riccardo Blumer |
| Materials | polyurethane foam and wood veneers |
| Manufacturer | Alias |
| Country | Italy |
| Date | 1996 |

'Laleggera' can be literally translated as 'the light one', and this chair amply deserves this description. The new manufacturing technique that made it provides an interesting marriage of materials not commonly used together.

## Volumes of production

This is a unique form of production so there are no points of comparison, nevertheless the manufacturers state that over 8000 chairs were produced in 2005.

## Unit price vs capital investment

This information was not made available, though it is fair to assume that a certain degree of experimentation would have been required in order that the process be set up. However, the materials (a combination of cut sheet material and injected foam) could be experimented with, in a very low-tech, cost-effective manner.

## Speed

Each chair requires four weeks to produce from start to finish.

## Surface

The surface finish available with this type of production is totally dependent on the plywood rather than the foam core. The surface of plywood varies depending on which type of wood is selected.

## Types/complexity of shape

The shapes are determined by the ability of the plywood to be cut and assembled into a hollow shell.

## Scale

The table, which is the largest piece in this collection, measures 240 by 120 by 73 centimetres.

## Tolerances

Information not available, but it can be assumed that the tolerances are governed by the plywood and its ability to respond to injected foam.

## Relevant materials

The chair uses a combination of plywood for the exterior structure and an internal structure of polyurethane foam.

## Typical products

The unique nature of the process means that the only products manufactured are chairs and a table. However, there is no reason why the principle could not be extended to include other objects that require strength and lightweight properties.

## Similar methods

This production method has been created by Alias in cooperation with the designer Riccardo Blumer. The manufacturers claim that there are no other production methods similar to this one. The nearest comparison contained in this book, though it produces a very different sort of product, is inflating wood (p.166).

## Further information

www.aliasdesign.it

1 The frame for a table is formed from a two-part male and female press.

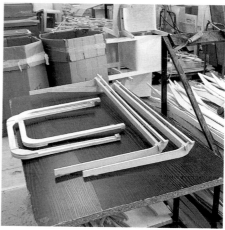

2 The formed components ready for assembly.

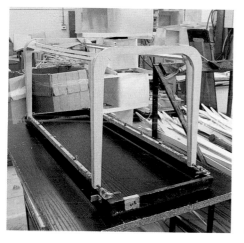

3 The structure of the table is made by gluing the formed components together.

4 Presses form the plywood around the table frame.

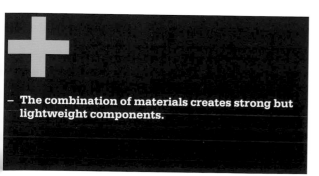

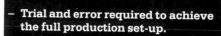

- The combination of materials creates strong but lightweight components.

- Trial and error required to achieve the full production set-up.

- Limited production base.

# Inflating Wood

Wood may have been one of the earliest materials used by humans to produce objects, but there are many new methods of forming and transforming various forms of this basic material into new states. Most wood is transformed by being attacked with blades, but the process discussed below is a much gentler way of forming wood that relies to a large extent on the individual pattern of the grain to control the final outcome.

The process of cross-grain laminating veneers of wood was invented by the ancient Egyptians; the technique of bending plywood to introduce curves developed far more recently; and the new process of inflating wood marks the next level of sophistication in wood forming techniques. Forming wood into compound curves has always been a costly and time-consuming process however, designer Malcolm Jordan has created a unique way of forming plywood into a series of undulating and controlled forms, though the secret of the process remains undisclosed.

The process started life as one of the many inspiring projects that have come out of the three-dimensional design course at Brighton University, on the south coast of England. Malcolm Jordan says, 'My background is in aviation. I am a licensed helicopter engineer and being surrounded by lightweight composite structures might have informed the line of experimentation. I tried a series

| Product | door panel |
| --- | --- |
| Designer | Malcolm Jordan |
| Materials | wood veneer with foam core |
| Manufacturer | Curvy Composites |
| Country | UK |
| Date | 2005 |

The undulating, compound, organic curves that are the result of this unique process allow thin wooden veneers to take on a visual quality that is perfectly suited to the natural tactile warmth of wood.

of experiments with various core materials between thin plywood skins.'

The eventual product is a composite structure, with plywood skins sandwiching a foam core. Areas of the plywood surfaces are clamped in a retaining jig. Expanding liquid foam is introduced, and the unretained surfaces move freely to form compound curves. The sizes of these wavy forms and the technique are not restricted to linear and parallel boards, but are based solely on the predetermined plywood stock sheet sizes.

## Volumes of production

Most suited to batch production, rather than high-volume mass-production.

## Unit price vs capital investment

Low capital investment and moderate unit cost when compared with similar methods (see below).

## Speed

Dependent upon the shape or product required – for example, in the case of a batch of wall panels, the skins and frames can be pre-assembled. The foam injection is a quick process, although the assembly can remain clamped in its retaining jig for up to eight hours to cure the foam. Output would therefore be accelerated with the use of multiple retaining jigs.

## Types/complexity of shape

Panels can be made either flat on one side and undulating on the other, or with two undulating surfaces that mirror each other. Because the plywood skins can be bent before the foam is injected, the process does not need to be restricted to linear or parallel boards. Solid inserts can be installed during production for 'hard points', for example to enable the attachment of legs or fittings, or to join sections together.

## Scale

The scale is restricted by predetermined plywood stock sheet sizes. It has the potential for use in furniture, but there is almost certainly the possibility of a myriad of sculptural and spatial applications for architectural and interior design purposes.

## Tolerances

Working with a natural material under pressure to freely form 'unnatural' three-dimensional shapes is not an exact process. Initially, there was difficulty in predicting the outcome of the curves, and the results were sometimes unexpected. However, when pressure points have been positioned and temperature and foam quantities are constant, visually similar results have been achieved.

## Relevant materials

Polyurethane expanding foam (there are variations with fire-retardant additives and versions without free icocyanates). Birch-faced aero-ply ranging in thickness from 0.8 to 3 millimetres.

## Similar methods

Deep three-dimensional forming in plywood (p.67) and foam moulding into plywood shells (p.163).

## Further information

www.curvycomposites.co.uk

1  A metal jig is set up that will hold the plywood panel.

2  Final preparation of the plywood before the introduction of the foam.

3  Finishing the moulded panel.

4  A cross-section of a sample showing the foam core.

**+**

- The resulting component combines lightness with strength, distributing the load through the plywood skins.

- High-impact resistance, with thermal and acoustic isolation potential.

- Removes the need for complex moulding techniques, hand carving or machining.

**–**

- Controlling the foam pressure. At present the quantity and pressure of the injected foam is regulated via inlet- and outlet-restricting devices, although experience has shown that the pressure created can be enough to rupture the plywood (with a big bang).

- Curving plywood can highlight flaws in the wood, often caused by manufacturing tools when the plywood's veneers were cut. Careful selection of plywood or a veneer added to the plywood overcomes this.

- Only available through one manufacturer.

# Forging
with open- and closed-die (drop),
press and upset forging

Forging is a major process in metal forming, sometimes utilising architectural-scale machines for pounding metals into shape. It is not only a method of forming metal, it also produces a change in its physical properties, resulting in enhanced strength and ductility. In its simplest manual form – open-die forging – it involves a chunk of metal being heated to just above its recrystallisation temperature and then being formed into shape by repeated blows with a hammer, as performed by a traditional blacksmith. Movement of the work piece is the key to this method. In its more industrial incarnation, it incorporates several variations, including hot and cold forgings.

Closed-die (or drop) forging involves a very similar process to that of the open-die method described above. In this instance, however, the shaped hammer is held in a machine

| Product | raw, semi-finished spanner |
|---|---|
| Materials | steel |
| Manufacturer | original manufacturer undisclosed, but finished by King Dick Tools in the UK |
| Country | Germany and UK |

This unfinished ring spanner is the result of the closed-die forging process and is seen here before it is finished by drilling with a pilot hole and broached with a serrated tool to obtain the twelve points.

and repeatedly dropped onto the metal, which sits in a shaped die. The shape of the two parts determines the formed shape. Drop forging can be either hot or cold. The hot form involves the blank metal being heated, and results in stronger components due to the realignment of the grain.

Press forging involves a heated bar being slowly squeezed between two rollers, which form the metal as it is fed through. Upset forging is used for shaping the ends of the rods by compressing them as they are held in the die. Typical products produced by upset forging are nails or bolts.

### Volumes of production
From simple hand forgings up to about 10,000 units.
### Unit price vs capital investment
In hot open-die forging, done by hand, the cost is based on the skilled manual labour. In automated methods, tooling costs can be very high.
### Speed
Quite slow, which is partly due to the fact that 90 per cent of all forging processes are hot processes, so that the work pieces need to be heated before forming.
### Surface
Forged parts will generally need to be machined in order to achieve a good, smooth surface and to remove flashing, which is the result of metal being squeezed out into a flat web around the outside of the part.
### Types/complexity of shape
The type of forging process will dictate the complexity and type of shape that is possible. In drop forging, draft angles are generally required, and parting lines need to be designed in order for complex shapes to be formed. Draft angles vary and are dependent on the type of metal used.
### Scale
Forging can be used for parts that weigh from a few grams to those reaching 0.5 tons.

### Tolerances
High tolerances are difficult to achieve, partly due to the wearing of the die. Different metals offer a range of tolerances.
### Relevant materials
With hot forging, most metal and alloys can be formed. However, the ease with which they can be forged varies enormously.
### Typical products
Because of the increased strength of forged components (compared with cast metals), a large number are used in aircraft engines and structures. Other applications include hand tools such as hammers, wrenches and spanners, and swords – notably Samurai swords.
### Similar methods
Powder forging (p.172). Impact extrusion (p.128) and rotary swaging (p.88) are both forms of forging.
### Further information
www.forging.org
www.iiftec.co.uk
www.key-to-steel.com
www.kingdicktools.co.uk
www.britishmetalforming.com

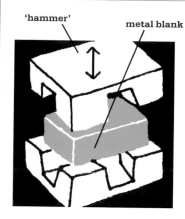
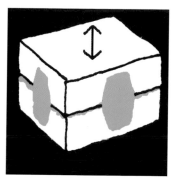
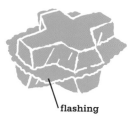

'hammer'

metal blank

flashing

1 In hot closed-die forging, a metal blank is heated and placed in a die cavity.

2 The male and female parts of the mould compress the metal, by means of a hammering action, into the die cavity.

3 The part is removed from the mould ready for the flashing to be machined away.

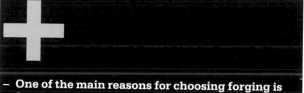

- One of the main reasons for choosing forging is for the control it gives over the grain structure in the metal. It allows for the grain flow to be aligned to specific shapes, making the part stronger and more ductile.

- No gaps or voids occur in the metal, as they can in die casting (see p.195) and sand casting (see p.202).

- Less waste than with runners and sprues.

- Forged parts often require machining to remove the excess metal that is left when the two halves of the die are brought together.

# Powder Forging
## AKA Sinter Forging

Powder metal forging is a process that sits within the realm of powder metallurgy. It combines sintering (see p.150) and forging (see p.169) to produce finished parts. As in other forms of powder metallurgy, the process begins with the forming of the metal powder into a 'green' state in a die. At this stage, the component is known as a 'pre-form', and is slightly different in shape from the final component. The pre-form is sintered to obtain a solid component, which is removed from the furnace, coated with a lubricant such as graphite, and transferred to a forging press. Here, the final component is formed in a closed-die forge, which forces the metal particles to interlock and become a solid, dense mass. The extra compaction provided by this process gives a highly dense, non-porous component.

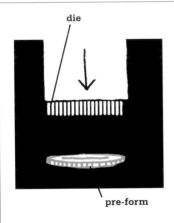

die

pre-form

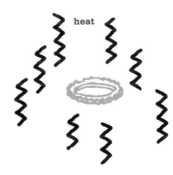

heat

1  Metal powder is compressed into a 'green' state in a die to obtain the preform.

2  The pre-form is sintered to obtain a solid component, which is removed from the furnace, coated with a lubricant such as graphite, and transferred to a forging press.

3  The final component is formed in a closed-die forge, which forces the metal particles to interlock and become a solid, dense mass.

**Volumes of production**
High volumes, typically over 25,000 units.

**Unit price vs capital investment**
This high-volume production process is expensive, partly because of the need for two sets of dies. Large volumes are needed to produce economical components.

**Speed**
Depending on the set-up and the component size, extremely high speeds are possible to achieve.

**Surface**
Good surface, which does not need secondary processing such as heat treating.

**Types/complexity of shape**
The process is capable of producing complex shapes. Powder forging can accommodate a high degree of varying wall thicknesses, which can be as low as 1 millimetre. Undercuts are not possible.

**Scale**
Similar to drop forging and press forging (for both, see forging, p.169) – think of a spanner or a gear (around 200 millimetres in diameter) for reference.

**Tolerances**
Part of the advantage of powder forging is its ability to produce parts with higher tolerances than other forging methods.

**Relevant materials**
Most ferrous and non-ferrous metals. A large number of powder forgings use iron with small amounts of copper and carbon.

**Typical products**
Engineering components for a range of industries, including automotive parts, connecting rods, cams, hand tools and transmission components.

**Similar methods**
Drop forging and press forging (p.169) and compression moulding (p.156).

**Further information**
www.mpif.org/DesignCenter/powder_forge.asp?linkid=43
www.gknsintermetals.com/technology/powder
www.ascosintering.com

— No gaps or voids in the metal, which can occur in, for example, sand casting (see p.202).

— Compared with other powder metallurgy processes, powder forging provides parts with greater ductility and strength.

— Efficient use of material, with less wastage than in other forms of forging (see p.169).

— Requires far fewer post-forming operations than other forging methods.

— Expensive tooling that requires large volumes of production.

# Precise-Cast Prototyping (pcPRO®)

The Fraunhofer Institute in Germany is one of the world's biggest research organisations concerned with materials and manufacturing. One method of production that has recently been developed by the institute is precise-cast prototyping.

Precise-cast prototyping (or pcPRO®) is a method for rapid prototyping that combines casting and milling operations in a single machine. It is a two-stage process, with the first stage involving a milling machine (see p.14) cutting a mould into an aluminium block using information from a CAD file. This mould is filled with a polymer resin. Once the resin has hardened, the same milling machine cuts it to a precise final shape. The essence of this process is that it allows for one side of a product (the moulded side) to be replicated exactly each time the mould is filled, but the top (milled) side may be adapted according to the information contained in the CAD file.

A product prototype usually requires numerous adjustments before it is optimised, forcing the modelmaker

| Product | sample components |
| --- | --- |
| Materials | polymer resin |
| Manufacturer | Fraunhofer Institute |
| Country | Germany |
| Date | 2004 |

These sample components, shown from both the top and underside surfaces, are an example of the machined CAD-cut details. The cutting lines on the surface are visible, as is the flat cast side.

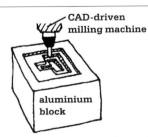
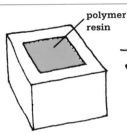

1  Information is used to generate a CAD file of the shape to be formed, which is fed into a milling machine, where the mould is cut into an aluminium block.

2  The mould is filled with a polymer resin.

3  Once the resin has hardened, it is cut to a precise final shape by the same milling machine.

4  The finished part is removed.

to start from scratch each time. With precise-cast prototyping, however, changes are only ever made in the CAD data. The main advantage is that for components such as housings for various electrical products, which have one side where the shape needs to be fine-tuned, multiples can be cast using the mould, with only one side being altered with CAD files.

**Volumes of production**
This is a CAD-driven process so it is suited to both one-off and batch production, though, obviously, the moulded side remains constant, so 'one-offs' only differ on their milled side.

**Unit price vs capital investment**
The tooling (the mould, in this case) is made using the same machine that makes the component, which means precise-cast prototyping is highly cost-effective.

**Speed**
Milling of the mould typically takes between half an hour and two hours; casting and curing of the resin and milling of each part takes a minimum of an hour, depending on the part's complexity.

**Surface**
The surface quality corresponds with the normal quality of milled surfaces.

**Types/complexity of shape**
The shape is limited only by the CAD drawing and the cutter (or cutters), though extremely complex shaped parts or undercuts in the inner contour can be made by five-axes milling only (that is, one cutter moving along five trajectories) and undercuts in the outer contour require special mould inserts or silicone parts.

**Scale**
The scale of the parts made on a standard machine is 250 by 250 by 150 millimetres.

**Tolerances**
Depending on the machine's accuracy, commonly some 10 microns.

**Relevant material**
A two-component resin.

**Typical products**
Complex shaped parts with high-tolerance outer surfaces and low-tolerance inner surfaces. The process is particularly useful for the rapid prototyping of bodies of mobile phones, cameras, automotive car parts, and electric and computer accessories.

**Similar methods**
Conventional milling (p.14) and casting methods. Other prototyping techniques, including stereolithography (p.218).

**Further information**
www.fraunhofer.de

- Permits the combination of automated and shape-specific manufacturing.
- Time- and cost-effective.
- High-quality finish.

- Limited number of manufacturers offer this method.

# 6:
# Compl

## Parts with complex shapes and surfaces

These processes can be described as 'plastic-state forming' because of the soft, malleable and, generally, hot state of the materials as they are moulded. It is these methods of production that are most responsible for the explosion in the number of cheap, moulded plastic products now available. Nevertheless, the payback for achieving complexity at a low cost per unit is the level of investment required for tooling. This chapter contains many of the established methods of high-volume mass-production, such as injection moulding in plastic and die-casting in metals. It also investigates methods of adding finishing materials to complex shapes.

# Injection Moulding
## with water injection technology (WIT)

Is injection moulding the mother of all plastic-processing techniques? It is through this process that we are able to transform plastic into a mass of packaging, toys and casings for electronics. It could well have been an injection mould that French philosopher Roland Barthes was referring to when he wrote, in his *Mythologies* (1957), of '. . . an ideally shaped machine, tabulated and oblong (a shape well suited to suggest the secret of an itinerary) effortlessly draws out a heap of greenish crystals, shiny and fluted dressing-room tidies. At one end, raw, telluric matter, at the other, the finished, human artefact, hardly watched over by an attendant in a cloth cap, half-god, half-robot.'

The process employs plastic pellets, which are fed from a hopper into a heated cylinder, which contains a screw. The screw carries the hot plastic, slowly melting it, and finally injecting it at high pressure into a series of gates and runners, which feed the polymer into a water-cooled steel mould. Once the part has solidified under pressure, pins eject the finished part from the mould.

Water injection technology (WIT), or water-assisted injection moulding, is a relatively new technology that promises several advantages over conventional injection moulding and gas-assisted injection moulding (see p.183). It is based on several variations, which either employ the injection of water to ram the melt (polymer) into the mould, or use water injection as a means of forcing the polymer outwards, to the walls of the mould, to create hollow parts. The use of water eliminates some of the problems that are associated with gas-assisted injection moulding, such as migration of the gas into the plastics. In addition, due to the fact that water cannot be compressed, a greater degree of pressure is produced than can be provided by gas, which results in several advantages in terms of the complexity and finish of the final parts. Faster cycle times are also achievable due to the cooling effect of the water.

| Product | **BIC® Cristal® ballpoint pen** |
|---|---|
| Designer | Marcel Bich |
| Materials | polystyrene (shaft); polypropylene (lid and plug) |
| Manufacturer | BIC |
| Country | France |
| Date | 1950 |

Fourteen million BIC biros are sold worldwide every day. All the elements of this iconic ballpoint pen are made using injection moulding, except for the cartridge and nib.

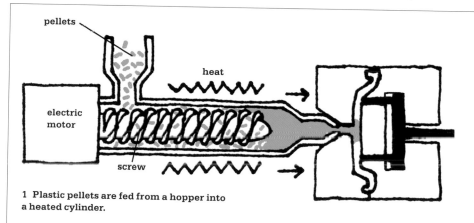

1 Plastic pellets are fed from a hopper into a heated cylinder.

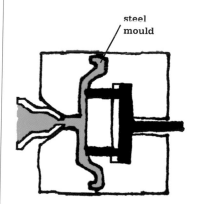

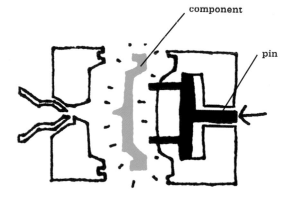

2 The screw injects the polymer into gates and runners, which feed into the steel mould where the component is formed.

3 The machine opens ready for ejection of the component by a series of pins.

### Volumes of production

Small injection-moulding manufacturers can be found to produce simple components of 5,000 units or less. However, the minimum quantity is generally accepted to be 10,000 units.

### Unit price vs capital investment

Unit price is very low, but this must be set against the high tooling costs, which can run into tens of thousands of pounds.

### Speed

Cycle times vary depending on the type of material, wall thickness and the geometry of the part. As an example, simple bottle tops have the fastest cycle times of between 5 and 10 seconds. A common speed for more complex parts is between 30 and 40 seconds.

### Surface

This is determined by the steel mould, and can vary from spark-eroded to highly glossy. The points where ejector pins are located in the mould need to be considered when designing a part, as these leave small, indented circles. Parting lines, where the various parts of the mould come together, also need to be considered.

### Types/complexity of shape

If the volumes of production are particularly great, injection moulding can be used to form highly complex parts. However, features such as undercuts, variable wall thicknesses, inserts and threads will add significantly to the cost of the tooling. Generally, injection moulding is suited to thin-walled sections.

### Scale

Micro-injection moulding is a specialist area and there are certain manufacturers who specialise in parts that are often less than 1 millimetre in size. For large-scale products such as garden chairs, it is worth considering gas-assisted injection moulding (p.183), and, where thick walls are required, try reaction injection moulding (RIM) (p.181).

### Tolerances

±0.1 millimetre.

### Relevant materials

Predominantly used for thermoplastics, but thermosets and elastomers can also be used.

### Typical products

It is impossible to state 'typical' products produced by injection moulding because its use is so widespread, from sweet packaging (tic tacs™ boxes, for example) to medical implants.

### Similar methods

The equivalent process for metals is metal injection moulding (MIM) (p.192) or high-pressure die-casting (p.195).

### Further information

www.bpf.co.uk
www.injection-molding-resource.org

- **Highly versatile in terms of moulding different shapes.**
- **Highly automated production.**
- **Cost-effective parts.**

- **Involves considerable investment and high production runs.**
- **Can involve long lead times.**

# Reaction Injection Moulding (RIM)
## with R-RIM and S-RIM

Reaction injection moulding (RIM) is a process that is used for producing structural foam components. Unlike standard injection moulding (see p.178), which uses pellets as the starting point, RIM involves feeding two reactive thermosetting liquid resins into a mixing chamber. They are then injected through a nozzle into the mould, where an exothermic chemical reaction produces a self-forming, smooth skin over a foam core. Depending on the formulation of the resin, parts produced using RIM can either be soft foams or solid, highly rigid components.

Composites can be produced by introducing short or long fibres into the mixture, to add reinforcement. This form of production can be broken down into two categories: reinforced-reaction injection moulding (R-RIM) and structural-reaction injection moulding (S-RIM).

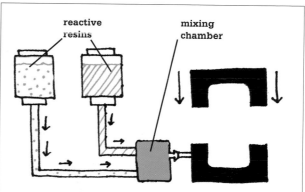

1  A combination of two reactive resins is fed into a mixing chamber.

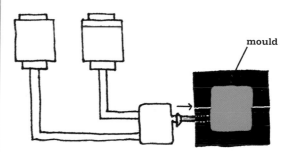

2  From this chamber the resins are fed into the mould, where an exothermic chemical reaction produces a smooth skin over the foam core of the final component.

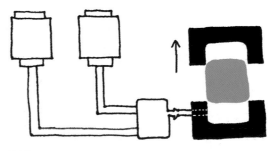

3  The cured part is removed from the mould.

### Volumes of production

Suited to high-volume production, however, because of the potential to use inexpensive, low-strength moulds, low-volume production is also a realistic possibility.

### Unit price vs capital investment

This is a low-pressure process with low tooling costs compared to those of standard injection moulding (see p.178). However, set-up costs are high, so large numbers of units need to be produced in order to be economical.

### Speed

This is not a rapid process, unlike standard injection moulding. Cycle times are considerably longer and, depending on the size and complexity of the part, can take several minutes, as opposed to seconds, per part.

### Surface

The foams produced using this process are 'self-skinning' and sometimes form a hard skin similar in quality to that formed in standard injection moulding, while retaining the foam core.

### Types/complexity of shape

Large and complex solid shapes are possible, with the potential to create varying wall thicknesses in the same component. Typical wall thicknesses of RIM parts are a chunky 8 millimetres.

### Scale

Suited to large-scale components up to 2 metres long.

### Tolerances

High tolerances.

### Relevant materials

RIM is often used to form dense polyurethane foams. Other common materials include phenolics, nylon 6, polyester and epoxies.

### Typical products

Large foam mouldings, rigid and flexible alike, are manufactured using RIM for use in products such as car bumpers and trim, industrial pallets, casings for large-scale electronics and refrigerator door panels.

### Similar methods

Injection moulding (p.178) and transfer moulding (p.158). Also, gas-assisted injection moulding (p.183), which allows for complex, large lightweight parts, although it is not suited to foams.

### Further information

www.pmahome.org
www.rimmolding.com
www.plasticparts.org

- Allows for varying wall thicknesses within the same part.
- Because of the low pressures and temperatures required for this process, tooling costs can be low compared with other high-volume plastic methods.
- Produces parts with a high strength-to-weight ratio.
- Suitable for making large parts.

- A multiple-cavity mould is needed for small parts.

# Gas-Assisted Injection Moulding

In standard injection moulding, thermoplastics are heated and injected into a mould (see p.178). Channels in the mould act to cool the plastic part before it is released from the mould. During cooling, the part shrinks and moves away from the walls of the mould and, to compensate for this, more material is injected into the mould.

An alternative to this widely used method is to inject gas, usually nitrogen, into the mould cavity while the plastic is still in its molten state. This internal force counteracts the shrinkage by inflating the component, forcing it to remain in contact with the surface of the mould until it solidifies, resulting in parts with hollow sections or cavities.

There are two types of gas-assisted injection moulding: internal and external moulding. The former is the most widely used, with the external method being used when greater definition in the part, or a larger surface area, is required. This is achieved by injecting a very thin layer of gas between one surface of the plastic and its adjoining mould cavity.

Exploiting the reduction in weight provided by this process, the Italian manufacturer Magis has produced a range of furniture that redefines the rules for designing large-scale plastic products. The ubiquitous low-grade garden chairs, produced by standard injection moulding, that you find in your local DIY retailer are made with a thin cross-section and have a strong, stable structure. By contrast, the Magis range, designed by Jasper Morrison, appears to be solid, but the inside is hollow.

| Product | Air-Chair |
|---|---|
| Designer | Jasper Morrison |
| Materials | polypropylene, with glass-fibre reinforcement |
| Manufacturer | Magis |
| Country | Italy |
| Date | 1999 |

This stackable chair, while sturdy enough to withstand considerable bulk, is lightweight, hollow and economical, all of which are the advantages of using gas-assisted injection moulding.

**Volumes of production**
Strictly a high-volume production process.
**Unit price vs capital investment**
Like standard injection moulding (see p.178), it combines low unit costs with high investment.
**Speed**
Due to the fact that material is injected only once and cools more quickly than it would in standard injection moulding, cycle times are reduced.
**Surface**
One of the key advantages of this form of injection moulding is the superior finish. During standard injection moulding, stress usually occurs along the flow line inside the mould, resulting in warping. The introduction of gas helps to distribute the pressure evenly and eliminate the stress and flow lines in the plastic at specific points.
**Types/complexity of shape**
Injection moulding is one the best methods of producing complex shapes, and gas-assisted injection moulding is no exception. Depending on how much you want to spend on tooling and the number of parts in the mould, you can achieve some highly complex shapes.

**Scale**
From casings for small electronic components to large pieces of furniture.
**Tolerances**
With greater control over the material and less shrinkage than in standard injection moulding, tolerances are higher.
**Relevant materials**
Most thermoplastics, including high-impact polystyrene, talc-filled polypropylene, acrylonitrile butadiene styrene (ABS), rigid PVC and nylon, and also composites.
**Typical products**
Virtually all mouldable parts can be made using gas-assisted injection moulding. External gas-assisted injection moulding is often used for components with large surface areas, such as car-body panels, furniture, refrigerator doors and high-end plastic garden furniture.
**Similar methods**
Injection moulding (p.178) and reaction injection moulding (RIM) (p.181).
**Further information**
www.magisdesign.com
www.gasinjection.com

- Allows for components to be made with variable wall thicknesses.
- Reduced cycle times.
- Reduced weight.
- Less sink marking than in conventional injection moulding (see p.178).
- Consumes 15 per cent less energy than standard injection moulding.

- Because of the extra parameters involved – the handling of gas, regulation of pressure and cooling – potential problems need to be addressed in advance, requires experience, and often, a fairly complicated set-up.

# Insert Moulding

Insert moulding is a branch of multi-component moulding (also called two-shot moulding), which is a method of combining different plastics in the course of only a single manufacturing process. Insert moulding refers to the stage of the process where parts (made from a variety of materials, including metal, ceramic and plastics) are inserted to increase strength in the plastic component. Injection moulding (see p.178) is the dominant element in this method of manufacture, with the inserts being placed in the mould prior to the injection of plastics.

Multi-component insert moulding using injection moulding exists in two forms. In the first method, known as rotary transfer, two materials are injected into the same mould cavity with the mould having been rotated between. The second method,

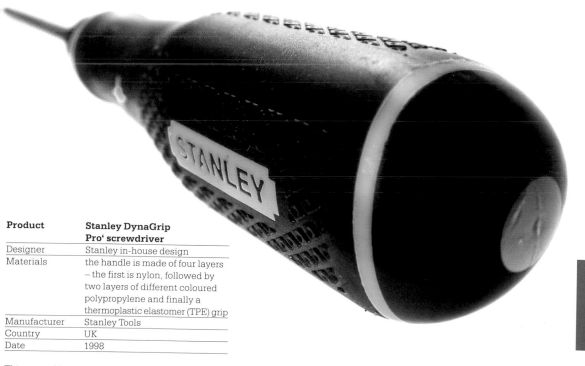

| Product | Stanley DynaGrip Pro' screwdriver |
| --- | --- |
| Designer | Stanley in-house design |
| Materials | the handle is made of four layers – the first is nylon, followed by two layers of different coloured polypropylene and finally a thermoplastic elastomer (TPE) grip |
| Manufacturer | Stanley Tools |
| Country | UK |
| Date | 1998 |

This screwdriver consists of four layers of plastic moulded over the metal shank: the first, blue moulding can be seen at the end of the handle; the shiny black area that fits into the palm of your hand is the second layer; the yellow graphics are the third; finally, the black grip.

commonly referred to as robot transfer, involves a component being produced first and only afterwards being transferred to another mould for a second material to be added.

There are also other forms of insert moulding that, instead of injection moulding, use compression (p.156 ), contact (p.134) and rotational (p.119) moulding.

## Robot Transfer Method

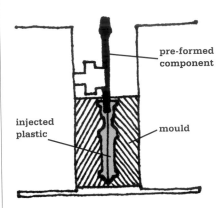

pre-formed component

injected plastic

mould

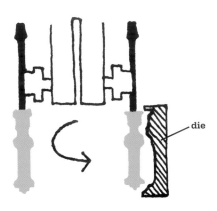

die

1  Plastic is injected over a preformed component, in this case the metal shaft of a screwdriver.

2  The moulded plastic part (together with the shaft) is removed by robotic arms and transferred into a separate die.

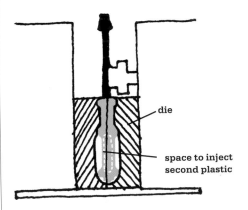

die

space to inject second plastic

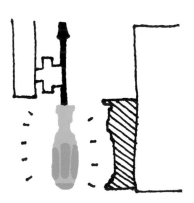

3  At this point, a second plastic is injected over the original moulding. This process can be repeated as many times as necessary to build up the required number of materials.

4  The finished component is removed from the mould.

**Volumes of production**
High-volume production process, typically above 100,000 units.

**Unit price vs capital investment**
An economical process when compared with manual assembly of the different materials.

**Speed**
Depends on the product. Thin-walled products cool very quickly, but the type of plastic and overall component design are also important factors.

**Surface**
Depends on the moulding process used, but is comparable to injection moulding (see p.178) but, in with insert moulding, surface materials may be introduced that can enhance the finish, for example the extra grip on a toothbrush handle.

**Types/complexity of shape**
Since this type of insert moulding is based on injection moulding, the same possibilities and restrictions apply, although the shape of the insert itself will partly dictate the shapes achievable.

**Scale**
It is possible to achieve products of greatly varying size depending on the type of injection moulding used.

**Tolerances**
Can be very high, because injection moulding can achieve tolerances of ±0.1 millimetre

**Relevant materials**
Any combination of materials, including thermoplastic and thermoset polymers. Depending on the combination of materials, different layers may bond chemically to varying degrees. However, thermosets and thermoplastic elastomers (TPEs), for example, generally do not provide a chemical bond.

**Typical products**
One of the key features of combining different materials is that you are able to bring together multiple functions in a single component. For instance, it is possible to have movable joints and decorative features over a flexible yet strong core, without the additional assembly costs. Typical products that are made through this process include toothbrushes, screwdrivers, razors and housings (of, for example, power tools with rubber grips).

**Similar methods**
In mould decoration (p.108).

**Further information**
www.engel.info
www.bpf.co.uk
www.mckechnie.co.uk

– Allows a range of differing physical and tactile properties to be incorporated into a single component.

– Reduced labour costs for assembly.

– Can add a whole range of increased functionalities.

– High tooling costs.

– Requires an advanced degree of knowledge on how to combine the various materials, and on subsequent design considerations such as shrinkage and the stresses of one material over another.

# In-Mould Decoration

As the name implies, this is not a method of production as such, but, rather, in-mould decoration was developed as an economical way of adding decorative surfaces to injection-moulded plastic parts. It offers a way of eliminating the necessity of having to print directly onto a part in a separate, post-forming process. This manufacturing technique is becoming more and more important with the growing market for electronic products, which makes increasing use of graphics for keypads, product branding and the personalising of portable consumer products.

The process begins with the printing of the graphic onto a polycarbonate or polyester film, known as a 'foil'. Depending on the shape of the component to be moulded, the foil is fed on a ribbon into the mould (or is cut and individually inserted, if the part is curved). The process is also suitable for shapes with compound curves, but in this case the foil needs to be moulded to shape before being inserted into the mould.

One of the uses for in-mould decoration is as an alternative to spraying or moulding parts in specific colours. It is a way of applying colour to products to ensure consistency between mouldings in different materials, where exact colour matches are hard to achieve. An example of the use of this process can be found in the back and front mouldings of a mobile phone, where the back is moulded in one material and the front in another.

| Product | Polar 8810i heart-rate monitor |
|---|---|
| Materials | Autoflex Hiform M polycarbonate film |
| Manufacturer | Polar |
| Country | UK |
| Date | 2000 |

In-mould decoration can be seen in the texture on the face of this monitor. A 'self-healing' film has also been used on the face of the monitor, which repairs small scrathes.

**Volumes of production**
Suited to mass-production.

**Unit price vs capital investment**
In-mould decoration is very cost-effective compared with painting or spraying parts in a separate process.

**Speed**
As you might imagine, inserting the film has a slightly negative effect on the overall cycle times, but this step can be automated and it needs to be considered in relation to the time it would otherwise take to decorate a part by, for example, painting it.

**Surface**
Different films can be used to give a variety of finishes ranging from the functional to the decorative.

**Types/complexity of shape**
In-mould decoration can be used on both simple and complex compound curves.

**Scale**
As injection moulding (see p.178). It is possible to make very small parts, but the shapes need to be very simple.

**Tolerances**
Not applicable.

**Relevant materials**
Polycarbonate, acrylonitrile butadiene styrene (ABS), polymethyl methacrylate (PMMA), polystyrene and polypropylene.

**Typical products**
In-mould decoration is not just limited to text-based graphics, but is also used to produce colour on mouldings and to add surface patterns. One of the most interesting (albeit invisible) foils that can be applied is a form of 'self-healing' skin. This protective layer helps to keep handheld products, such as mobile-phone casings, shiny and free from scratches. Other applications include decorative mobile-phone covers, machine fascia, digital watches, keypads and automotive trim, to mention just a small selection of products.

**Similar methods**
Over-mould decoration (p.190) is similar, but involves the application of materials, rather than foils, to a moulding. Sublimation coating is another alternative, although it is applied as a secondary process after moulding and is particularly suited to engineering polymers such as nylon.

**Further information**
www.autotype.com.sg
www.filminsertmoulding.com

- Cost-effective to customise parts and provide customer differentiation without re-tooling.

- Allows for virtually any colour, image and, even, surface texture to be added as a skin.

- Equally suited to short and long production runs.

- Films can be used to offer surfaces that are scratch-, chemical- and abrasion-resistant.

- Incurs additional moulding costs because of the complexity of the mould required to accommodate a film or foil.

# Over-Mould Decoration

Over-mould decoration is not really a method of production in is own right, but rather an extension of standard injection moulding (see p.178), as part of a two-step process. What is particularly noteworthy about it is that it can give plastic components an almost craftlike quality by the way it cleverly allows a different material to cover the plastic in the mould.

If you were to see a mobile-phone casing, for example, that has a small patch of fabric wrapped onto its surface, you might find it an interesting combination and imagine that the addition of the fabric would require a whole new process involving someone fixing the fabric by hand onto the plastic moulding. In reality, this would be labour-intensive and expensive. Inclosia Solutions, a branch of Dow Chemical, has come up with the technology to combine plastic with a range of other materials during the moulding process itself, eliminating the need for any secondary finishing.

The benefit of this type of manufacturing is that it provides designers with a new set of materials, surfaces and finishes to challenge traditional notions of plastic-moulded products. Instead of electronic products having the same all-over plastic skin, they can have warm, tactile surfaces that are closer to textiles or to crafted

| Product | E-Go laptop |
|---|---|
| Designer | Marcel van Galen |
| Materials | fabric over a plastic moulding |
| Manufacturer | Tulip |
| Country | The Netherlands |
| Date | 2005 |

The internal plastic moulding of this laptop computer can be over-moulded with a range of different materials to suit varying consumer markets. The leather and fabric 'skins' allow for consumer electronics to be marketed in the same way as more fashion-led products, such as handbags.

materials such as wood. The process offers the possibility of extending our perception of products beyond the current boundaries of identical, mass-produced plastic, making it feasible for products to be 'dressed' and become more integrated with our clothes, furniture and jewellery.

**Volumes of production**
High-volume production process.

**Unit price vs capital investment**
Unit price for components is more than that for standard injection moulding (see p.178). Tooling costs are higher due to the need to incorporate a second material.

**Speed**
Because it is a two-step process that involves forming a material over a pre-formed component, it is slower than some similar methods of multi-component (that is, two-shot) moulding.

**Surface**
The key feature here is that it allows for secondary 'skins' to be applied over plastic mouldings, so the surface is determined by the material you choose as the covering.

**Types/complexity of shape**
Because of the secondary material, over-mould decoration is best suited to flat surfaces and those with a deep draw.

**Scale**
The largest standard size is approximately 300 by 300 millimetres.

**Tolerances**
Depend on the shrinkage of the various materials.

**Relevant materials**
A variety of thin materials can be used to over-mould, such as aluminium sheet, leather, fabric and thin wooden veneers.

**Typical products**
Over-moulding has been used in a range of products that fall into the category of personal mobile technology, including mobile phones, Personal Digital Assistants (PDAs) and laptop computers.

**Similar methods**
In mould decoration (p.188) and insert moulding (p.185).

**Further information**
www.dow.com/inclosia
www.filminsertmoulding.com

**+**
- Automated method of covering plastic-moulded components with a second soft, or decorative, material.
- Cost-effective alternative to hand assembly.
- Compatible with most engineering thermoplastics and elastomers.

**−**
- Although over-moulding provides benefits when it comes to surface decoration, it is a two-step process, adding to unit price.
- Can require trial and error when using untested materials.

# Metal Injection Moulding (MIM)

A variation on standard injection moulding (which uses plastics; see p.178), metal injection moulding (MIM) is a relatively new way of producing complex shapes in large numbers from metals that have a high melting point, such as tool steel and stainless steel that would not be suitable for high-pressure die-casting (see p.195). The process is limited by the suitability of the metal powders that are used as the raw material, which need to be particularly fine.

MIM involves more processes than plastic injection moulding, because of the necessity of adding binders to the metal. The various companies involved in using this technology each have their own unique binder systems but typically

| Product | engineering components [pen nib for scale only] |
|---|---|
| Materials | low-alloy steel and stainless steel |
| Manufacturer | Metal Injection Mouldings Ltd, part of PI Castings |
| Country | UK |
| Date | first produced in the UK in 1989 |

This range of small-scale, complex engineering components is typical of the type of products that are made using MIM. It offers us the chance to create precise, solid metal products from metals with high melting points that cannot easily be formed by casting. The strength and hardness of these components offers several advantages over other forms of metal production.

the binders, which can account for 50 per cent of the compound, are made from a variety of materials, including wax and a range of plastics. They are mixed in with the metal powders to produce the moulding compound.

Once the shapes have been moulded, the binder is no longer needed and is removed from the metal particles. What is left is then sintered (see p.150), which shrinks the component by about 20 per cent.

### Volumes of production

In order to justify the set-up and tooling costs, high-volume production is needed – a minimum of 10,000 units.

### Unit price vs capital investment

High capital investment but a very low unit price.

### Speed

The actual injection of material is similar to that of standard injection moulding in plastics (see p.178), but the sintering and the removal of the binder add time and expense to the process.

### Surface

The process gives an excellent surface finish on components and has the ability to produce fine detail.

### Types/complexity of shape

Highly complex shapes similar to those obtainable through standard plastic injection moulding. These can also be enhanced by the use of multi-cavity tooling.

### Scale

MIM is currently capable of producing only small parts for use in larger products.

### Tolerances

The MIM process can achieve a general tolerance of ±0.10 millimetres.

### Relevant materials

MIM is economical for producing large numbers of complex components with a range of surface finishes. It can be applied to a range of metals: bronze, stainless steel, low-alloy steels, tool steels, magnetic alloys and alloys of low thermal expansion.

### Typical products

Surgical and dental tools, computer components, automotive parts, casings for electronics and consumer products (mobile phones, laptops, PDAs).

### Similar methods

Although die-casting in metal (p.195) is possibly the closest to MIM in terms of production quantities and complexity of shape achievable, the key difference between the processes is in the ability of MIM to work with metals with high melting points, such as low-alloy steels and stainless steel.

### Further information

www.mimparts.com
www.pi-castings.co.uk
www.mpif.org

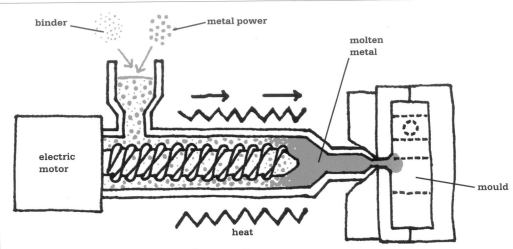

binder — metal power

molten metal

electric motor

heat

mould

1  Binders are mixed with metal powders to produce the moulding compound. This is fed into the injection-moulding machine to form a 'green' component.

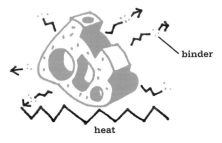

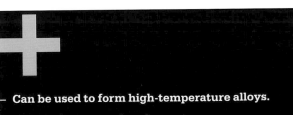

binder

heat

2  After the shape has been moulded, the binder is removed from the metal particles and discarded. This step is achieved in a number of ways depending on the specific manufacturer.

3  What is left is sintered to weld the metal particles together. This shrinks the component by about 20 per cent.

**+**

- Can be used to form high-temperature alloys.
- Used to form complex shapes.
- Cost-effective for large numbers.
- No post finishing required.
- Parts have exhibited good strength.

**—**

- Low overall part size.
- Compared with standard injection moulding in plastic (see p.178), only a limited number of manufacturers can offer MIM.

# High-Pressure Die-Casting

High-pressure die-casting is one of the most economical methods of producing metal components with complex shapes. It is the process to use if you want to produce high volumes of intricate components. In this sense, it is similar to metal injection moulding (MIM) (see p.192), but its main advantage over MIM is that it is suitable

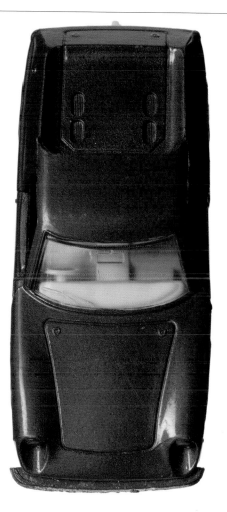

| aProduct | Matchbox 'Lotus Europa' |
|---|---|
| Materials | zinc |
| Manufacturer | Matchbox |
| Country | UK |
| Date | 1969 |

Die-cast metal toys are part of many people's childhood memories. The ability of die-casting to create fine, complex details is well illustrated by the clearly legible text on the underside of my son's toy car.

for metals with low melting-points where no sintering is required.

The process involves molten metal being poured into a reservoir, where a plunger forces the liquid, under high pressure, into a die cavity.

The pressure is maintained until the metal solidifies, at which point small ejector pins push the components out of the die. Just as in injection moulding (see p.178), die-casting moulding dies are made in two halves.

### Volumes of production

High-pressure die-casting is strictly for high-volume production.

### Unit price vs capital investment

Economical unit price is obtained by mass-producing highly complex parts, which eventually drives down the relative cost of the expensive tooling that has to be designed to withstand repeated injection of molten metal at high pressure.

### Speed

Fast, although the removal of flashing as a separate process adds to the time.

### Surface

Excellent.

### Types/complexity of shape

Ideal for producing complex, open-walled parts in metal, especially those with thin wall sections. Unlike investment casting (see p.198), high-pressure die-casting requires draft angles.

### Scale

Up to a maximum weight of approximately 45 kilograms for an aluminium component.

### Tolerances

Reasonably high level of tolerance, but shrinkage can sometimes be problematic.

### Relevant materials

Metals with a low melting temperature, such as aluminium and zinc, which are by far the most commonly used materials. Others include brass and magnesium alloys.

### Typical products

Chassis for a range of electrical products such as PCs, cameras, DVD players, furniture components and wet-shaver handles.

### Similar methods

Investment casting (p.198) and sand casting (p.202), which allow the casting of larger parts and require les capital investment, but demand higher tolerances. Gravity die-casting is a much older process and is employed on a much smaller scale of production than high-pressure die-casting.

### Further information

www.castmetalsfederation.com
www.diecasting.org

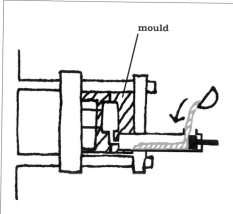

1  Molten metal is poured into a reservoir.

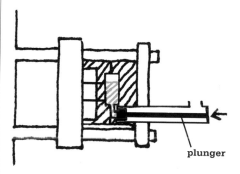

2  A plunger forces the liquid under high pressure into a die cavity.

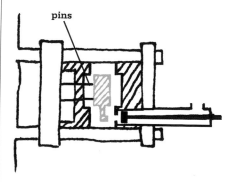

3  The pressure is maintained until the metal solidifies, at which time small ejector pins push the components out of the die.

- Ideal for complex shapes.
- Excellent surface finish.
- Good dimensional accuracy.
- Can allow for small sections and thin walls.
- Excellent consistency between parts.
- A fast process that requires minimal post-machining work.

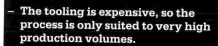

- The tooling is expensive, so the process is only suited to very high production volumes.
- Produces parts where flash is present.
- Parts are not guaranteed to have high structural strength.

# Investment Casting
## AKA Lost-Wax Casting

The name 'investment casting' is taken from the idea that the process involves 'investment' in a sacrificial material, and it is characterised by its ability to produce highly complex shapes. The process has been around for thousands of years, with evidence of its use by the ancient Egyptians. In essence, it involves a wax shape being dipped into a ceramic liquid which itself forms a thick enough skin to hold molten metal once the wax has been melted away. Because the ceramic mould is broken to reveal the finished object, it is possible to get away with all kinds of undercuts and complex shapes that would not be possible to achieve with a rigid mould.

The first stage involves the manufacture of a die (usually made

wax pattern                    ceramic shell                    finished product

| Product | 'Spirit of Ecstasy' car hood ornament |
| --- | --- |
| Designer | Charles Robinson |
| Materials | stainless steel |
| Manufacturer | Polycast Ltd |
| Country | UK |
| Date | 1911 |

These images illustrate three of the stages of investment casting for this highly recognisable figure. They also offer an excellent example of which method of production to choose when the fashion for ornate, decorative figurines returns to contemporary design.

from aluminium, but a polymer can also be appropriate), which is repeatedly used to obtain the wax replica patterns. Multiple patterns are produced that are assembled onto a wax runner, which forms a structure that resembles a kind of tree. This assembled runner is then dipped into ceramic slurry, which is dried to form the hard ceramic skin. The dipping is repeated until sufficient layers have been built up. The runner is then placed in an oven to melt the wax so that it can be poured out before the ceramic is fired. The ceramic shells are now strong enough to allow molten metal to be poured into them. After cooling, the ceramic can be broken away and each part may be removed from the tree inside.

## Volumes of production

Depending on size, it is possible to have several hundred small parts on a tree, which can be cast in one pour. Larger items are made with only one per tree. Investment casting is a process that allows for small runs of below a hundred, as well as runs of up to tens of thousands.

## Unit price vs capital investment

The tooling is far cheaper than that needed for high-pressure die-casting (see p.195), which means lower capital investment. Depending on the size of the final component, multiple castings can be produced on the same tree to increase cost-effectiveness.

## Speed

Slow, requiring a number of steps to be completed for each component.

## Surface

Good surface finish, but this is largely dependent on the surface of the pattern.

## Types/complexity of shape

Unlike in high-pressure die-casting, which requires draft angles, components made by investment casting can be highly complex. This is the main advantage the process has over other methods of forming.

## Scale

Anything from 5 millimetres to about 500 millimetres long, or up to 100 kilograms.

## Tolerances

High.

## Relevant materials

A wide variety of ferrous and non-ferrous metals.

## Typical products

Anything from sculptures and statues to gas turbines, marine shackles, jewellery and medical tools. One example with an extremely high profile is the 'Spirit of Ecstasy' that sits on the bonnets of Rolls-Royce cars.

## Similar methods

High-pressure die-casting (p.195), sand casting (p.202) and centrifugal casting (p.143).

## Further information

www.polycast.co.uk
www.castmetalfederation.com
www.castingstechnology.com
www.pi-castings.co.uk
www.tms.org
www.maybrey.co.uk

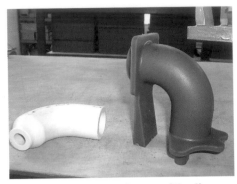

1  After the initial manufacture of the die, a wax pattern (on the right) is produced.

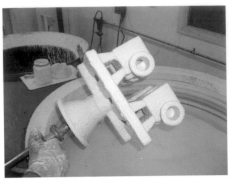

2  This image, featuring a different pattern, shows a simple set of four components being dipped into the ceramic slurry.

3  A typical set-up showing a number of wax components on a simple runner before being dipped into the slurry.

4  The ceramic shell filled with metal (with a finished component held next to it for comparison).

5  This is the stage where the dried ceramic is removed and discarded revealing the final component.

6  A final component shown with the original wax pattern.

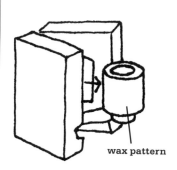

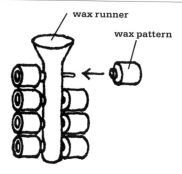

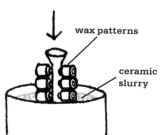

wax runner

wax pattern

wax patterns

ceramic
slurry

wax pattern

1  Wax patterns are made using an aluminium die, which is reused to obtain the required number.

2  The individual wax patterns are assembled onto a wax runner.

3  The assembled runner is dipped into ceramic slurry and dried to form the hard ceramic skin. The process is repeated until sufficient layers have built up.

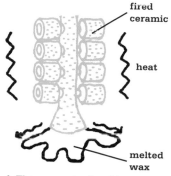

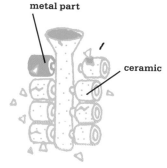

fired
ceramic

heat

metal part

ceramic

melted
wax

4  The runner is placed in an oven to melt the wax so that it can be poured out before the ceramic is fired.

5  Molten metal is poured into the fired ceramic shells. After cooling, the ceramic is broken away and each metal part can be removed from the tree inside.

6  The finished casting.

- Complex shapes with hollow cores are possible.

- Weight savings due to the ability to form hollow cores.

- A process for high accuracy.

- Eliminates post-process machining operations.

- Freedom of design.

- Involves several stages.

- Some foundries still use alcohol-based binders in the shell, which may pose a threat to the environment.

# Sand Casting
## including CO₂ silicate and shell casting

Of the many attributes of sand, one that stands out is the fact that it is a refractory material. This means that it can withstand extremely high temperatures, and thus easily accommodate molten metals for casting. There are various forms of sand casting, the differences lying mainly in the quantity of the components that is required, but all rely on the very simple principle of making a pattern (or duplicate) of the finished part. This duplicate is embedded in a compacted mixture of sand and clay and then removed, leaving a cavity into which a molten metal can be poured. Runners and risers are used in the sand to contain a reservoir of excess molten material. These are, essentially, holes in the sand: the runner allows metal to be poured in; the riser holds any excess molten metal. This is a necessary precaution, because as molten metal solidifies, it shrinks, and at this stage excess metal is drawn into the mould to prevent voids in the casting.

There are several derivatives of this basic principle. These include the use of patterns made from sacrificial materials such as polystyrene foam, which evaporate when the metal is poured in. Wooden patterns are used for small-batch work in foundries, while the process can also be automated in a procedure that uses aluminium patterns and a programmed compaction method.

Other methods include CO₂ silicate casting and shell casting. The CO₂ process is a recent development,

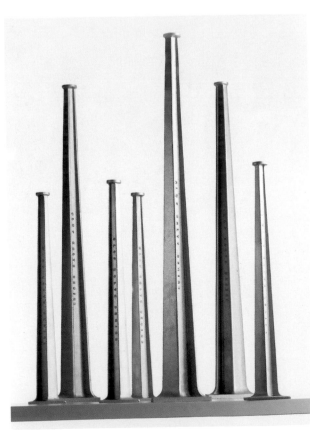

| Product | 'High Funk' table legs |
| --- | --- |
| Designer | Olof Kolte |
| Materials | aluminium |
| Manufacturer | First produced by David Design |
| Country | Sweden |
| Date | 2001 |

The concept behind these table legs is that the design is sold without a table-top, so that customers can buy legs to fit under the table-top of their choice.

and it involves the sand being bonded with sodium silicate instead of clay. This is converted into $CO_2$ during casting and it can provide greater accuracy because sodium silicate makes a tougher mould. Shell casting uses fine-grained, very pure sand, coated in a thermosetting resin. This means that the mould can be thin walled (as little as 10 millimetres) but it is very strong. Shell casting offers several advantages over conventional sand casting, such as greater tolerance and a smoother surface.

### Volumes of production

Sand casting can be used to make a single component or in large production runs.

### Unit price vs capital investment

For manual sand casting, the price is dependent on the cost of making a wooden pattern, with the unit price of the component being relatively cheap. Automated processes are expensive, but will obviously produce lower unit costs.

### Speed

Compared to high-pressure die-casting (see p.195), this is a fairly time-consuming process.

### Surface

Casting in sand gives a surface that is very textured and that needs to be ground and polished if a fine surface is required. Sand casting using polystyrene leaves no parting lines and thus requires less finishing. Shell casting can also provide a greater surface finish.

### Types/complexity of shape

By its nature sand is a fragile material to cast with, which means sand casting is best suited to quite simple shapes. However, the large number of processes that has developed allows for the production of complex shapes with varying wall thicknesses and undercuts.

### Scale

Compared with other forms of metal casting, sand casting allows for the casting of very large components, but parts require a minimum of 3 to 5 millimetre wall thicknesses, and they have a comparatively coarse finish.

### Tolerances

As is the case with many other casting techniques, it is important to take shrinkage into account when considering the process. Various metals will have different shrinkage rates, but generally no more than approximately 2.5 per cent. Shell casting provides a higher level of dimensional accuracy.

### Relevant materials

As a general rule, metals with low melting points, such as lead, zinc, tin, aluminium, copper alloys, iron and certain steels.

### Typical products

Car engine blocks, cylinder heads and turbine manifolds.

### Similar methods

Comparable, but more expensive, methods include die-casting (p.195) and investment casting (p.198), but on the whole sand casting is capable of producing more intricate shapes.

### Further information

www.icme.org.uk
www.castingsdev.com
www.castingstechnology.com
www.engineersedge.com/sand_cast
www.engineersedge.com/casting_design

1 The cavity in the bottom mould is clearly visible as the top is lowered.

2 Molten metal is poured into the runners.

3 The part is lifted off with the top mould, ready for finishing.

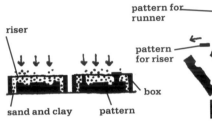

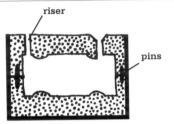

1 First, the original pattern (which includes the runners and risers) is embedded in each of the two halves of the sand box.

2 Once the sand has been compacted, the pattern is removed.

3 The two halves of the sand box are brought together and secured with aligning pins.

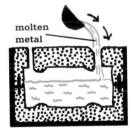

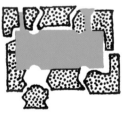

4 Molten metal is poured into the runners, filling the mould cavity.

5 Once the casting has cooled, the part is pulled from the sand.

6 The finished part.

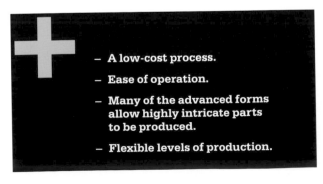

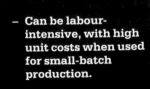

- A low-cost process.

- Ease of operation.

- Many of the advanced forms allow highly intricate parts to be produced.

- Flexible levels of production.

- Can be labour-intensive, with high unit costs when used for small-batch production.

- Parts may require a lot of finishing.

# Pressing Glass

Described as the closest thing to 'injection moulding for glass', the pressed glass process makes it possible to mass-produce intricate glass products with detailing on the inside, as well as the outside, of the shapes. This is in marked contrast to glass blowing (see p.98), in which detailing is restricted to the outside surface only. It is possible to trace the staggering boom in the mass-production of all kinds of inexpensive glass products back to the introduction of pressed glass in 1827.

The core of the process involves male and female moulds that are carefully preheated and maintained at a steady temperature to ensure that the hot glass will not stick to the moulds. A gob of gummy, molten glass is squashed between the two moulds, with the amount of space left between the male and female parts determining the thickness of the final component. It is these two moulds – which produce an inner and outer imprint – that allow the shape to be controlled on two surfaces. In large-scale production, the machines typically work on a turntable with a number of stations performing the various stages of production, from filling the mould with glass to the actual pressing.

| Product | lemon squeezer |
| --- | --- |
| Materials | soda-lime glass |
| Country | China |

Along with pub ashtrays, this lemon squeezer – bought from my local supermarket – illustrates the complex, thick and chunky-walled forms that can be achieved by machine pressing glass in contrast to thinner, hollow, machine-blown glass products.

The thick-walled, chunky products that this process tends to produce are much more utilitarian than fine quality cut glass, which goes through a secondary process of grinding to achieve the crisp, sharp edges that are its hallmark. As in the case of other processes that generate products with a strong character, the particular 'look' and 'feel' of pressed glass has led to some pieces becoming collector's items.

## Volumes of production

Glass pressing is a term that can be applied to a hand process, a semi-automated or an automated machine process. Semi-automated production can be used for a minimum of 500 units, and is often employed for sampling large production runs for fully automated production.

## Unit price vs capital investment

In fully automated production, the unit prices can be extremely low, but like most high-volume production, it requires expensive tooling.

## Speed

In an automated set-up, and depending on the component size, a single machine can be set up to hold several moulds at the same time. This can result in huge production rates – some approaching 5,000 pieces per hour.

## Surface

Dimples, serrations and diamond patterns are all achievable in pressed glass, although the definition is less pronounced than such patterns in cut glass.

## Types/complexity of shape

While blown glass (see p.98) lends itself well to rounded shapes, pressed glass is a lot more versatile because it allows for more complex detailing and decoration. One of the key design features to bear in mind is that it is not possible to have a closed shape and, as in thermoforming (see p.53), the component must have a draft angle to allow for the mould to open at the end of production. Pressed glass is also more suited to thick-walled hollow ware.

## Scale

Some semi-automated production allows for a maximum of about 600 millimetres in diameter. Larger pieces can be made, depending on the volume of production and the manufacturer.

## Tolerances

Due to contraction and expansion of the material, glass pressing is able to match the high tolerance of engineered components. However, a typical tolerance is ±1 millimetre.

## Relevant materials

Almost any type of glass.

## Typical products

Lemon squeezers, railway signal lamps, lenses, street and display lighting, laboratory glass, pub ashtrays, pavement lenses, wall blocks, marine and ship lighting, aircraft and airport runway lenses, and road and traffic signals.

## Similar methods

Cut glass can be used for fine-detailed patterns, but this is really your best bet for producing open glass shapes with the potential for decoration on both sides. For plastic components, you might want to consider compression moulding (p.156).

## Further information

www.nazeing-glass.com
www.glasspac.com
www.britglass.org.uk

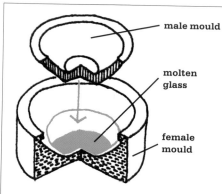

1  The male and female moulds are preheated and maintained at a steady temperature to ensure that the hot glass will not stick to the moulds.

2  The gob of gummy, molten glass is squashed between the two moulds. The thickness of the final component is determined by the amount of space left between the male and female moulds.

male mould

molten glass

female mould

– Definition can be achieved on both the inner and outer surfaces.

– Allows for surface detailing that might not be possible with blowing.

Its main disadvantage compared with blown-glass products (see p.98) is that it does not permit closed container shapes to be produced.

– Not suitable for making thin-walled sections.

– Generally involves more expensive tooling than that used in the mass-production of blown glass.

# Pressure-Assisted Slip Casting
## with pressure-assisted drain casting

Pressure-assisted slip casting is a development of conventional ceramic slip casting (see p.122). Compared with the traditional form, it offers several manufacturing advantages that affect the speed and complexity of the final component. Conventional slip casting involves the use of plaster moulds into which the ceramic 'slip' is poured. The 'de-watering' of this slip is based on a capillary action that draws water from the slip into the plaster, leaving the clay to form a dry layer against the internal wall of the mould. This can be quite slow and the plaster moulds have a limited life.

In pressure-assisted slip casting, a more resilient material, with larger holes, is used for the mould. The size of the holes means that the capillary action is reduced and replaced by the use of pressure (typically between 10 and 30 bar, depending on the size of the product). This involves pumping the slip into the porous plastic mould. Under this pressure, the water seeps out through naturally occurring capillary tubes in the mould. Once dried, the form is taken out of the mould and any imperfections are cleaned off. The product is then dried in fast dryers and sprayed with a glaze before firing.

A project called Flexiform, led by Ceram Research in the UK, has enhanced pressure-assisted slip casting, coming up with a process it calls 'pressure-assisted drain casting'. In this development, the conventional synthetic mould is replaced by a machinable plastic, which can be machined directly from the product designer's original CAD drawing. This offers a number of further advantages, including cheaper tooling and the possibility of the mould being re-cut, which is not possible with the moulds used for pressure-assisted slip casting.

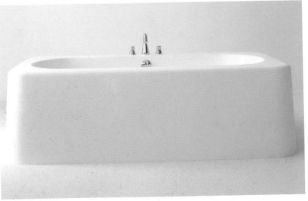

| Product | bath from the 'Loo' range |
|---|---|
| Designer | Marc Newson |
| Materials | ceramic |
| Manufacturer | Ideal Standard |
| Country | UK |
| Date | 2003 |

This bath is a typical example of the scale of casting that can be produced in ceramic.

### Volumes of production

Pressure-assisted slip casting moulds typically require volumes of approximately 10,000 pieces to justify the use of the plastic tooling.

### Unit price vs capital investment

Cost-effective unit parts, which are the result of several factors, outlined above. In the Flexiform pressure-assisted drain-casting project, mould costs are significantly reduced.

### Speed

Conventional slip casting (p.122) can require anything up to an hour for casting, de-moulding and drying. Pressure-assisted slip castings can typically result in a reduction in time of 30 per cent.

### Surface

Superior quality finish compared with conventional slip casting, with reduced casting seams resulting in less felting than with the conventional method.

### Types/complexity of shape

From small and simple to large and complex parts with undercuts. Anything, from bathroom products to art objects and dinnerware, can be made using this process. Just think of the U-bends on the underside of a toilet to glean an understanding of the types of complexity possible.

### Scale

From small teacups to toilets and baths.

### Tolerances

As is the case with any fired piece, moulds need to be made that take account of a reduction in size once the product has been fired.

### Relevant materials

Suited to most types of ceramic material.

### Typical products

Complex tableware, which can require four-part moulds for teapots and coffee pots with integral handles. Apart from its large-scale use in sanitary ware, it is in the area of advanced ceramic technology that pressure-assisted slip casting is attracting the strongest interest.

### Similar methods

Ceramic slip casting (p.122) and compression moulding (p.156).

### Further information

www.ceramfed.co.uk
www.ceramcunic.net
www.ceram.com
www.ideal-standard.co.uk

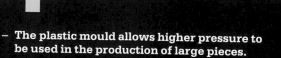

**+**

- The plastic mould allows higher pressure to be used in the production of large pieces.

- Plastic moulds have a longer life (approximately 10,000 casts) before they are thrown away.

- Fewer moulds are needed and less storage is required.

**–**

- The moulds add to the set-up costs (however, for drain casting, Flexiform moulds greatly reduce the tooling costs).

# Viscous Plastic Processing (VPP)

As the technology behind materials and manufacturing techniques progresses, the previously barren spaces between different families of materials are bridged. Of all the material families, plastics make up the group that is the most versatile in terms of production techniques available. However, other materials, such as metals and ceramics, are all being explored to find new ways of mass-producing components using plastic-state forming techniques. This allows materials that have traditionally limited means of forming, including ceramics, to be formed using methods such as injection moulding (see p.178).

The material and the method of production go hand in hand in the sense that the properties of the materials dictate the complexity of production that is available. One of the problems in forming ceramics involves

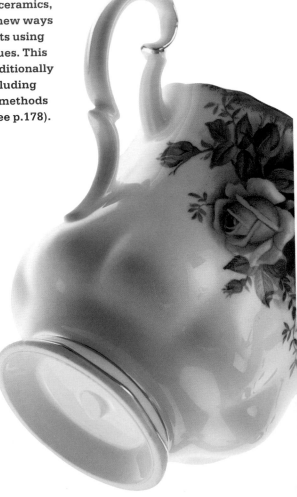

| Product | teacup from the 'Old Roses' range |
| --- | --- |
| Designer | Harold Holdcroft |
| Materials | bone china ceramic |
| Manufacturer | Royal Doulton |
| Country | UK |
| Date | 1962 |

VPP technology was used to enhance the properties of bone china, so that these uniquely British teacups could be injection moulded. A combination of design and the cost-effectiveness of this process means that 100,000,000 cups have been sold since 1962.

the need to eliminate the inherent microstructural defects in ceramic materials. These defects reduce the strength of the material, making it brittle. Viscous plastic processing, or VPP, is a method of enhancing the properties of ceramic materials that eliminates these flaws, resulting in a way of processing ceramics that is much more flexible and, to use the technical term, 'plastic' in its nature. The process involves ceramic powders being mixed with a viscous polymer under high pressure. This mixture can then be used to form components through a range of fabrication techniques, including extrusion (see p.78) and injection moulding.

**Volumes of production**
Not applicable.
**Unit price vs capital investment**
Not applicable.
**Speed**
Not applicable.
**Surface**
An excellent surface can be achieved, depending on the grain size of the ceramic powder.
**Types/complexity of shape**
Because of the enhanced 'viscous elastic behaviour' of ceramics produced in this manner, components have high strength in their 'green' state, which enables quite adventurous forms to be produced. The process also allows thinner wall sections to be produced than is the case with standard ceramic materials, which ultimately leads to higher strength parts with reduced weight.

**Scale**
It is possible to create large products, but not in all dimensions. VPP is, in other words, capable of producing long, extruded sections with wall thicknesses of up to 6 millimetres, or thin sheets.
**Tolerances**
Not applicable.
**Relevant materials**
Any ceramic material.
**Typical products**
Flat components, substrates for electrical components, kiln furniture, springs, rods and tubes, strength in green-state cups, body armour and biomedical applications.
**Similar methods**
Not applicable.
**Further information**
www.ceram.com

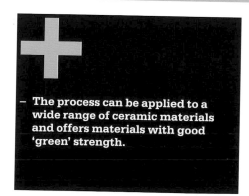

– The process can be applied to a wide range of ceramic materials and offers materials with good 'green' strength.

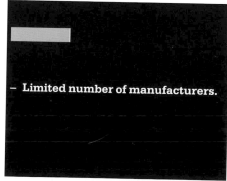

– Limited number of manufacturers.

# 7: Advan

# ed

## Advanced and new technologies

The starting point for most of the processes featured in this section is that the information used to make the shape is supplied by a CAD file. This eliminates tooling costs, as do Smart Mandrels™, also featured in this section (though these are not driven by CAD), and together they all provide a complete mind shift from existing rules of production. On this basis, the methods in this section point the way to future industrial production and hint at the fact that these new technologies will provoke the biggest change in the nature of mass-produced objects since the Industrial Revolution. It is a group of processes that includes the relatively familiar process of stereolithography, but also has some new technologies that put manufacturing into the hands of the consumer.

# Inkjet Printing

Desktop printers have allowed anyone with a computer to turn a desk into a place where all sorts of things can happen. The seemingly humble printer may well be the hub of a revolution that will change the way we make objects. The day will soon come when we will be able to download plans for a product (a door handle, for example) and make it from our own desktop three-dimensional printer, which has been loaded with the appropriate raw materials, in the same way that you load up your bread-maker last thing at night so that you can enjoy a fresh loaf in the morning. Before such three-dimensional technology becomes a reality at a domestic level, however, 'techies' are busy pushing the envelope to discover new applications for this familiar object, with its clanking robotics.

Already, Homaro Cantu, a chef based at Moto's restaurant in Chicago, has turned a Canon i560 inkjet printer into a machine for making food. Having replaced the ink cartridges, he prints edible liquids instead of CMYK inks onto an edible starch-based paper. In a move worthy of Willy Wonka (let's not forget the edible sugary grass and flowers in his chocolate factory), Cantu has abducted a printing process to create an entirely new concept in how you order – and what you can eat – in a restaurant.

Possibly one of the most unusual adaptations of this technology is one that has been developed by various teams of scientists across the world, who use 'modified' inkjet printers to build up living tissue. Based on the long-held knowledge that, when placed next to each other, cells will weld together, the process involves tissue being built up, using a thermo-reversible gel as a kind of scaffolding over each cell. The team that

| Product | edible menu |
| --- | --- |
| Designer | Homaro Cantu |
| Materials | vegetable-based dyes on edible paper |
| Manufacturer | Moto Restaurant, Chicago |
| Country | USA |
| Date | 2003 |

This printed edible menu provides an example of an interesting crossover between the food and the production industry and shows that even on a 'techno' level food is providing a rich source of experiments.

developed this, from the Medical University of South Carolina, uses the thermo-reversible gel as a way to support the cells as they are being distributed through the 'printing' action. This gel is interesting in itself, since it is designed to change instantly from liquid to gel (and back again) in response to a stimulus such as change in temperature.

### Volumes of production
From one-offs to small batch production.

### Unit price vs capital investment
Two-dimensional printers are within most people's budget, so you can take one apart and play with it at will, substituting the inks with anything you care to try.

### Speed
Depends on what you want to do, but typically this is still a fairly slow process.

### Surface
When making three-dimensional objects from standard production materials, the surface may have a ribbed texture as witness to the way the material has been laid down.

### Types/complexity of shape
Highly complex shapes, restricted only by what you draw on your computer.

### Scale
The team from the Medical University of South Carolina has demonstrated the highly controlled, cell-by-cell scale that is possible.

### Tolerances
The production of three-dimensional living tissue demonstrates the fine tolerances that are achievable.

### Relevant materials
Again, the machine is there to be explored, though you will need a basic combination of liquid and solid materials. The examples mentioned above give you some idea of the potential.

### Typical products
The beauty with this process is that the examples mentioned above are currently a sort of DIY production, based on groups of people tinkering with technology and machines to give them new functions. The two contrasting examples illustrate that there is no such thing as a typical product for this hybrid technology.

### Similar methods
Contour crafting (p.216), selective laser sintering (SLS) (p.224) and electroforming for micro-moulds (p.222).

### Further information
www.motorestaurant.com

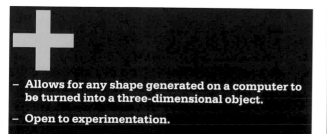

- **Allows for any shape generated on a computer to be turned into a three-dimensional object.**
- **Open to experimentation.**

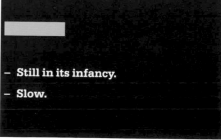

- **Still in its infancy.**
- **Slow.**

# Contour Crafting

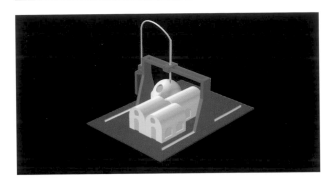

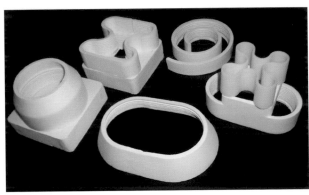

| Product | contour-crafted prototypes and CAD design drawing |
|---|---|
| Designer | developed by Dr Behrokh Khoshnevis |
| Materials | concrete |
| Manufacturer | Dr Khoshnevis, under National Science Foundation and Office of Naval Research |
| Country | USA |
| Date | expected to be commercially available in 2008 |

These samples, though not on the scale of a building, illustrate the types of forms that can be created through contour crafting. Above is an example of the sort of CAD design that will drive the spraying process.

This is a process that has the potential to revolutionise the construction industry. Dr Behrokh Khoshnevis, of the University of Southern California, has invented a machine that 'prints' houses. As he points out, the automation of the manufacturing industry has been advancing steadily ever since the Industrial Revolution. In comparison, developments in the construction industry have been meagre during the same period. However, this is something that Dr Khoshnevis plans to change with a process he calls 'contour crafting', an advanced form of spraying concrete.

Planned to be commercially available in 2008, the machines that are at the heart of this technology use a method of depositing concrete that is similar to that used in inkjet printers (see p.214) and extrusion (p.78). In this case, however, the technology is on a much larger scale, and it includes the ability of the 'printing' head to move in six axes and build up material in layers, based on CAD drawings rather than on two-dimensional graphics.

The 'printing' nozzles, which are suspended from an overhanging carriage, deposit quick-drying concrete, that is shaped by an integral trowel using a cylinder-and-piston system. A secondary feature of contour crafting is that the system allows utilities, such as conduits for electricity, plumbing and air-conditioning, to be embedded into the process.

**Volumes of production**

The key feature of contour crafting is that it is an automated building method, however buildings can, of course, only be erected one at a time.

**Unit price vs capital investment**

Allowing for the fact that multiple houses can be built using a single machine, Dr Khoshnevis estimates the cost of building an average-sized American house at between a fifth and a quarter of the current cost of building a house by conventional means.

**Speed**

Construction using this process can build a 2,000 square-foot house, including electricity and plumbing, in less than 24 hours.

**Surface**

The use of the various types of trowel produces a good concrete surface, one that requires no preparation before painting. A painting system may even be incorporated within the contour crafting process itself.

**Types/complexity of shape**

The shape is limited only by the CAD drawing and the normal physical forces that apply to buildings, though even shapes such as arches can be extruded through the nozzle.

**Scale**

Dr Khoshnevis suggests that this method can be used for anything from a small house to a high-rise structure.

**Tolerances**

The nozzle assembly that can move in six axes allows for very high tolerances on a large scale.

**Relevant materials**

Cement, with additives such as fibre, sand and gravel.

**Typical products**

This is a process that is offering the building industry a new way to construct permanent houses, buildings and complexes, as well as temporary emergency shelters.

**Similar methods**

On this scale, the process is unique. The CAD-based system makes it similar to many smaller scale rapid-prototyping processes (see, for example, stereolithography, p.218).

**Further information**

www.contourcrafting.org
www.freeformconstruction.co.uk

- Allows for rapid construction.
- Plans and designs can be easily altered because they are CAD-driven.
- It is possible to use local materials as reinforcement for the cement.
- Cost-effective.
- Automated process.

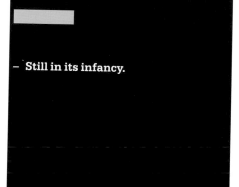

- Still in its infancy.

# Stereolithography (SLA)

Stereolithography (SLA) is one of the best known methods of rapid prototyping. Driven by a CAD file, components are produced by a laser, which scans a bath of photosensitive resin, building the components layer by layer. The ultraviolet laser beam is focused onto the surface of the liquid, tracing the cross-section of the part and turning successive thin layers of the liquid into solid. The solid part remains below the surface of the resin throughout the process, because it is seated on a bed that is lowered gradually, allowing the component to be built up in layers.

All rapid prototyping technologies give a geometrical freedom that no other processes do. SLA is typical in that it allows for the testing of components before entering into mass-production. Your choice of

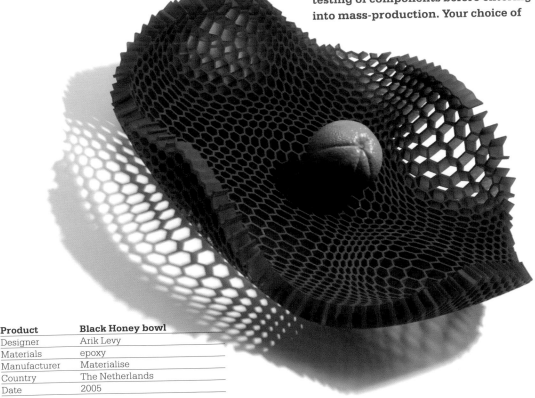

| Product | Black Honey bowl |
|---|---|
| Designer | Arik Levy |
| Materials | epoxy |
| Manufacturer | Materialise |
| Country | The Netherlands |
| Date | 2005 |

This beautiful, open-cell structure is an excellent example of the highly intricate and complex forms that can be built up using this process.

process is dependent on the geometry of the part, the surface quality required or the material that you want to use. Selective laser sintering (SLS) (see p.224), for example, cannot match SLA for quality.

SLA is an accurate process, although not the most accurate, and it can be applied to a range of materials, although not to as many as vacuum casting. (This is a method of producing small batches of identical components that are generally used for prototyping or modelmaking. It involves producing an original master that is cast into a silicone mould. The mould is subsequently filled with plastic resins. A vacuum is applied and the resulting parts are very accurate, with fine detail and thin wall sections.)

## Volumes of production
Due to the time it takes to build up a product, SLA is strictly limited to low-volume production.

## Unit price vs capital investment
No tooling, and, even with a fairly high unit price, it is still the most cost-effective way of making prototypes.

## Speed
Dependent on a number of factors, including the volume of the part, the material used, and the fineness of the step that is set by the operator. Another factor is the orientation of the component: if, for example, a drinks can is made lying down, the process is quicker, although less accurate, than when it is made standing up, which requires more passes with the laser.

## Surface
The 'stepping effect' as a result of the layering can be controlled by the thickness of the step. Also, shallow gradients will produce lines similar to contour lines on maps. Steep gradients and vertical walls will have smoother surfaces, but in both cases the part may need sand blasting.

## Types/complexity of shape
Anything that can be drawn on a computer.

## Scale
Standard machines can allow for a 500 by 500 by 600 millimetre building area. For anything bigger than this the components must be made in several sections and joined together. However, some companies make their own machines, producing components several metres long.

## Tolerances
Height is the least accurate dimension, because of the increased number of passes that the laser has to make, but tolerance is generally ±0.1 per cent plus 0.1 millimetre.

## Relevant materials
Ceramic, plastic or rubber can be used. More commonly, engineering polymers such as acrylonitrile butadiene styrene (ABS), polypropylene and acrylic mimics are used.

## Typical products
The word 'typical' has no application here, since you can make anything you want.

## Similar methods
Vacuum casting (see above), selective laser sintering (SLS) (p.224) and inkjet technology (p.214).

## Further information
www.crdm.co.uk
www.materialise.com
www.freedomofcreation.com

1  This image, of designer Patrick Jouin's CI chair, shows the finished product being raised from the liquid polymer. During actual production the only part visible is the very top edge of the chair as it is formed by the laser.

2  The finished chair is seen this time with a white block that acts as an internal support for the seat during the forming process, without which the chair would collapse.

3  The completed chair before removal of the support block.

4  The finished chair in all its translucent, ghostlike glory.

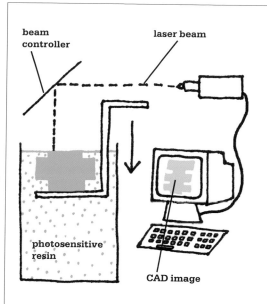

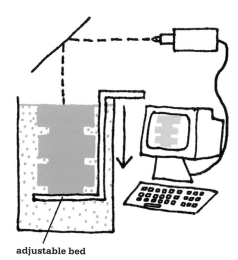

1  Driven by a CAD file, components are produced layer by layer by a laser scanning a bath of photosensitive resin.

2  The ultraviolet laser beam is focused onto the surface of the liquid, tracing the cross-section of the part and turning successive thin layers of the liquid into solid. The part gradually sinks below the surface as it is lowered in a bed, allowing the whole structure to be built up.

- Unlimited geometric freedom.

- Good surface finish.

- No intermediate steps between the CAD model and finished object.

- High unit costs.

- Only photosensitive resins can be used.

- Inaccuracy in two directions.

- Often needs support structures.

- Not as rapid as many other prototyping processes.

# Electroforming for Micro-Moulds

Swiss company Mimotec, has developed the process of electroforming (see p.146) to the extent that it can be used to make micro-moulds. Before describing the Mimotec process itself, however, I need to make it clear that micro-moulding is not the same as 'miniature' injection moulding. Micro-moulding is closer to the seriously minuscule nano-end of the scale, rather than just small-scale moulding, with parts being produced that can weigh as little as a few thousandths of a gram with details that measure only a few microns thick.

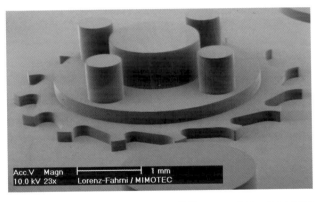

Although the principle behind micro-moulding is reasonably conventional, the methods used to produce the moulds are rather fascinating. Micro-moulds can be made by a number of different methods, including a micro-milling technique (where material is cut away). Mimotec, however, has harnessed the fine detailing achievable with electroforming to produce the most minute of moulds.

The Mimotec process starts with an unpolymerised layer of photo resist deposited on a glass plate. This is then exposed to ultraviolet light through a mask of the final shape, which causes the exposed resist to polymerise, leaving the non-exposed area to be washed away. The remaining part is coated with gold followed by a further layer of resist. The part is built up in this way to produce a more complex part, which acts as the moulding block and incorporates holes through which plastic for the component can be injected. This process is just one of many new methods of forming nano-scale components, and it is an excellent demonstration of the ever-advancing research that is going on in this field of production engineering.

| Product | micro-mould |
| --- | --- |
| Manufacturer | Mimotec |
| Country | Switzerland |

A close-up image of the finished part (top) shows the scale achievable, as does the mould (beneath) that has a pinion cavity of only 0.6 millimetres and a micro-inscription on the side. The plate (as the presence of the needle demonstrates) is only 5 by 9.8 millimetres, and 1.2 millimetres thick.

## Volumes of production

Production runs of up to tens of thousands of components are possible using this type of micro-mould.

## Unit price vs capital investment

The CAD-driven nature of this process means that the set-up costs are low.

## Speed

It takes about seven hours to deposit a layer 100 microns thick, but several thousand micro-moulds can be made concurrently on a single glass plate.

## Surface

It is possible to achieve high levels of detail and a fine finish on micromoulds made in this way.

## Types/complexity of shape

It is not possible to make moulds that are capable of making shapes with tapered, or anything other than straight vertical, sides. Steps can be produced but require longer timings.

## Scale

It is possible to create blocks of as little as 100 cubic microns, with embedded channels 30 microns wide. The largest parts are 100 by 50 millimetres.

## Tolerances

± 2 microns.

## Relevant materials

The micro-mould itself is made from gold with a nickel alloy coating. The moulded parts are generally made from polyacetals (POM) and acetal resins.

## Typical products

As you might expect, the micro-moulds are used to produce very small parts for biomedical devices and electronics, watch making and telecommunications components.

## Similar methods

Wire EDM (p.38) and micro-milling techniques.

## Further information

www.mimotec.ch

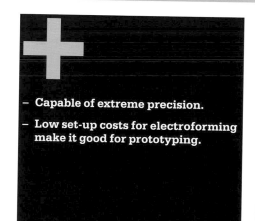

- **Capable of extreme precision.**
- **Low set-up costs for electroforming make it good for prototyping.**

- **Making micro-moulds in this way is a fairly slow process.**
- **Restrictions in current technology mean that only nickel and phospho-nickel alloys can be used for the micro-moulds.**

# Selective Laser Sintering (SLS)
## with selective laser melting (SLM)

Innovation in production techniques has recently been dominated by advances in rapid prototyping. Designers are increasingly able to exploit the potential to make unique objects directly from a CAD file on a computer and selective laser sintering (SLS) is just one of the significant developments, opening up a world of rapid prototyping.

Sintering (see p.150) is a significant part of the field of powder metallurgy and it can be used in a number of different production methods. Selective laser sintering is an adapted (and refined) form of sintering in which a laser is used to solidify precise areas in a powder block in order to produce lightweight components. As in any sintering process, a powdered material (in the case of the implants illustrated here, a metal) acts as the starting point. A laser, driven by a CAD file, is fired repeatedly into the powder, fusing the particles together layer by layer until the specific component is built up. The process is also known as selective laser melting (SLM) for obvious reasons.

This, however, is only the beginning for the team at Mining and Chemical Products Ltd in the UK who use the technology to produce a type of microscopic scaffolding. They are able to exploit the design potential of a CAD file to produce components with a tiny, but complex, lattice-like structure. This results in forms that are made up mainly of air, like a

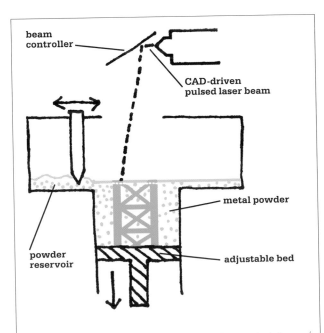

beam controller

CAD-driven pulsed laser beam

metal powder

powder reservoir

adjustable bed

A laser is fired repeatedly into a particulate material, fusing the particles together at the point of impact until the specific component is built up, layer by layer.

sponge. The advantage of this type of micro-scaffolding is that it enables components to be produced in metals with a very high strength-to-weight ratio – the density of stainless steel parts, for instance, can be reduced by as much as 90 per cent compared with conventional processes.

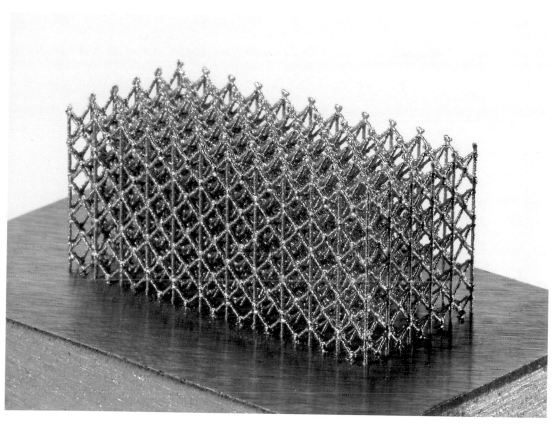

| Product | sample of a hierarchical structure produced using SLM technology |
|---|---|
| Designer | not applicable |
| Materials | stainless steel |
| Manufacturer | Mining Chemical Products Ltd Tooling Technologies |
| Country | UK |
| Date | 2005 |

This structure, only 3 centimetres high, was produced to demonstrate the small scale of work that is achievable using selective laser melting (SLM) technology.

**Volumes of production**
Each component is made individually.

**Unit price vs capital investment**
No tooling, but the unit price is high because parts are individually made.

**Speed**
Although it is anticipated that selective laser sintering will eventually be taken up more widely for end production, it is still a fairly slow and low-volume process best suited to prototyping.

**Surface**
Components currently show a surface roughness of 20–30 microns – very little, in other words.

**Types/complexity of shape**
Limited only by the CAD technology that drives it, the microstructure of the Mining and Chemical Products components demonstrates that this is about as good as it gets when it comes to creating complex shapes.

**Scale**
It is possible to achieve very fine details, such as thin vertical walls with a thickness of as little as a tenth of a millimetre, while the overall size of parts is limited by the size of the powder block reservoir that the machine can hold.

**Tolerances**
Extremely high.

**Relevant materials**
Any particulate material used in powder metallurgy: metals, including steel and titanium, and plastics.

**Typical products**
SLS, principally a form of rapid prototyping, was initially used to test models before production. However, designers are pushing the technology towards production of finished products. This particular technology can be used to make anything from jewellery and heat sinks for computers to medical and dentistry implants.

**Similar methods**
Other CAD-driven technologies including deposition prototyping (contour crafting, p.216, for example), stereolithography (p.218) and three-dimensional printing (such as adapted inkjet printing, p.214).

**Further information**
www.mcp-group.com/index.html
http://blogs.zdnet.com/emergingtech/ ?p=104

- Allows lightweight components with high strength to be produced.
- Easily customisable.
- Can be used with a range of metals and other materials.
- Fully automated system.

- High unit costs.

# Smart Mandrels™ for Filament Winding

Shape-memory alloys and polymers are big news in the world of materials. Characterised by their ability to be 'programmed' to a particular shape, once heated and softened they can be bent out of this shape and re-formed into a new shape, which is retained once the material has cooled. The clever part is that when reheated, the part will return to its original 'programmed' shape.

The US-based company, Cornerstone Research Group, one of the major world players in shape-memory technology, has exploited such materials to develop a patented tooling system, Smart Mandrels™, for producing mandrels for the process of filament winding (see p.140). This system can be used in two ways.

In the first case, a single-shape memory mandrel can be formed into a specific shape, used to produce the relevant components, and then reheated, re-formed and reused to form a new shaped mandrel for an entirely different component. The second application is in the forming of a complex mandrel, one that might otherwise have been impossible to remove from inside the final component because of undercuts, and so on.

Filament winding using Smart Mandrels™ means that the filament can be wound around the mandrel, which is subsequently heated, softened and returned to its 'programmed' straight tube shape. This allows the completed filament winding to be easily removed.

1 Winding onto the purple Smart Mandrel™ begins.

2 The Smart Mandrel™ is heated and softened for easy removal from the completed winding.

## Volumes of production

For now, small runs and prototyping only, but this recently developed process will be equally suitable for large-scale production, since the mandrels are durable and can be used to make many parts.

## Unit price vs capital investment

Smart Mandrels™ offer big savings for low production runs. This is because there is no need for expensive, multi-piece tooling, with the price staying at the same level for large production runs.

## Speed

Cycle times are several minutes for each part, but it is significantly quicker than conventional filament winding with rigid mandrels (see p.140) because there is no need to assemble and disassemble the mandrel for each part.

## Surface

No post finishing necessary, but the parts do have the distinctive 'look' of filament-wound products.

## Types/complexity of shape

The main advantage with Smart Mandrels™ is that they allow for more complex forms to be produced using the filament-winding process. These can incorporate undercuts and returns that would normally be impossible to produce, because the mandrel could not be removed from the component.

## Scale

Machines can be built to produce filament windings to a massive scale. The only limitations on scale will be the size at which the shape-memory alloys and polymers can be made and remain effective.

## Tolerances

Not the kind of process that is suitable when high tolerances are required.

## Relevant materials

Any thermoset plastic material, and glass or carbon fibre.

## Typical products

Aeronautical components, tanks, rockets and housings.

## Similar methods

Pultrusion (p.81), and contact moulding (hand or spray lay-up) (p.134).

## Further

www.crgrp.net/mandrels-processes.htm

- Capable of producing highly versatile shapes.
- Reduced labour costs due to the ease with which the mandrel can be removed.
- Reusable and adaptable tooling.
- Simple to remove mandrel from component.

- All parts have the distinctive 'look' of filament-wound products.
- Limited availability because it is a patented process.

# Incremental Sheet-Metal Forming

One of the major research areas in manufacturing at the moment is in the arena of 'industrial craft', a term that embraces a range of technologies that allow for a very flexible approach to mass-production by eliminating the need for specialised tooling. Incremental sheet-metal forming has the potential to revolutionise sheet-metal forming, making it available for low volumes of production for customised parts.

In essence, incremental sheet-metal forming is a type of rapid prototyping for sheet metal using a mobile indentor, so that almost any three-dimensional shell-shape can be made, without the need for specialised tooling. It is a term used to describe a number of methods of sheet forming that employ a generic, single-point tool that presses against a metal sheet in three axes (the work piece is held in a clamp), depressing it into a shape based on a path that is supplied by a CAD file.

The process has been in use for 15 years, but its potential is still not widely adopted in industry, chiefly as a result of the difficulty in assuring geometrical precision in the formed

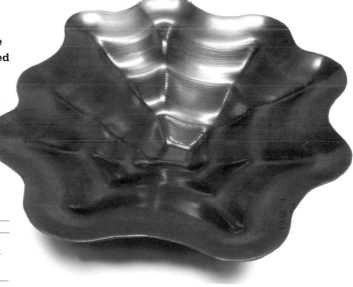

| Product | sample of incrementally formed sheet. |
|---|---|
| Materials | stainless steel |
| Manufacturer | sample produced by Institute for Manufacturing, Department of Engineering, University of Cambridge |
| Country | UK |
| Date | 2006 |

Researchers Julian Allwood and Kathryn Jackson of Cambridge University are two of the many researchers internationally who are looking at ways of developing the process for wider industrial use. The stepping that can be seen in this sample illustrates the path of the tool as it traces a path across the metal sheet slowly pushing it into shape.

## Volumes of production

The process of incremental sheet-metal forming is increasingly well known and is attractive because it offers the possibility of economic production of small batches. It has been used for manufacturing prototype products, including a prototype car made by Toyota. Other applications such as dental prosthetics, where each product must be unique, are also emerging.

## Unit price vs capital investment

The obvious advantage of this process lies in the fact that it allows low-volume production with extremely low tooling and set-up costs.

## Speed

Typical feed-rates can be up to 50 millimetres per second, and a typical part will take between 20 minutes and an hour, depending on the surface quality required.

## Surface

Depends on the step size between successive passes of the tool. A step size of around 0.1 millimetre per pass gives an A-class surface, as rated by a car body maker. The surface can also be enhanced by the use of moulds.

## Types/complexity of shape

Depends on whether or not a die is used, but the parts will always be shell-shaped – although, in the near future, machines will be built with upper and lower indentor tools to get around this.

## Scale

While typical components are approximately 150–300 millimetres square with an average thickness of 1 millimetre, researchers in Japan are capable of forming parts that range from a few millimetres long up to sheets that are 2 metres long.

## Tolerances

Depend on whether or not a die is used. First-time geometric accuracy can be poor (out by 2–5 millimetres), even if the tool path is only creating simple contours from a CAD model. This can be improved, but it involves trial and error. Accuracy is obviously much greater if a die is used.

## Relevant materials

A wide range of materials, including a selection of aluminium and steel alloys, stainless steel, pure titanium, brass and copper.

## Typical products

Several applications exploit the potential of this process for one-off production, including the manufacture and repair of car body panels, tailored medical devices and prosthetics, and architectural panels.

## Similar methods

Incremental sheet-metal forming has its roots in metal spinning (p.48), but obviously has far greater advantages in terms of rapid prototyping and flexible manufacturing. Another closely linked process is press forming (see metal cutting, p.51).

## Further information

www.ifm.eng.cam.ac.uk/sustainability/
  projects/incremental

part. However, Toyota has explored the process for forming parts for prototyping cars, using a one-sided die in order to gain more control.

There are a number of researchers exploring different variations of the process, some of whom are using two indentor tools at the same time, on either side of the work piece. Negative and positive dies can also be employed to give greater control of geometrical accuracy and surface finish.

This close-up image shows the single-point tool poised over the clamped sheet of metal, which is about to be formed into shape.

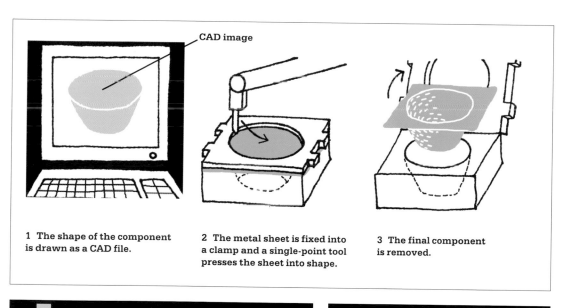

1 The shape of the component is drawn as a CAD file.

2 The metal sheet is fixed into a clamp and a single-point tool presses the sheet into shape.

3 The final component is removed.

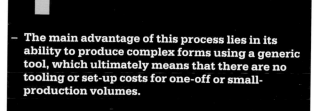

**+**

– The main advantage of this process lies in its ability to produce complex forms using a generic tool, which ultimately means that there are no tooling or set-up costs for one-off or small-production volumes.

**–**

– Limited availability.
– Still in its infancy.

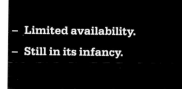

# Glossary
# Credits
# Index